The Care and Feeding
of
Your Aspie

by Kristopher Hoffman

Contents

Dedication

This is book is dedicated to the people in my life that "get me" ***and*** to all of those who don't but make an effort to be my friend anyway.

Introduction

What you hold in your hand is the effort of an Autistic Spectrum Disorder (ASD) individual to help. It is intended to be a translation guide to help Neurotypicals navigate the waters surrounding their ASD friends, loved ones and family members.

The Title:
The title of this book, *"The Care and Feeding of Your Aspie"* was intended to be funny, relevant and tongue in cheek. The impetus behind it was that, often, ASD individuals are viewed as something completely different and almost alien by the Neurotypicals around them. As such, special care and instructions are needed. If it offends you, that was not my intent.

What this book is:
It is a collection of essays written to facilitate Neurotypical/Autisic interractions. Each essay was written with the input of psychiatric professionals, input from several ASD adults and personal experiences. Each of the essays covers a topic that was recommended by friends and family and the community at www.wrongplanet.net. These essays are designed to help understand the mechanisms behind many common issues and behaviors you will encounter when dealing with ASD individuals.

It is an effort to help you understand us, to help us understand ourselves, and in some cases, help us understand you.

What this book is NOT:
This book is not an exhaustive guide. It is not backed by scientific studies into my essays. It is not definitive in any way. That is to say – this book is written from my personal understanding, and cannot, in any way, include the experiences and opinions of all ASD individuals. Nor does it claim to.

What I have done to prepare this book for printing:

I have done very little, honestly. These essays were originally published on my blog and shared with the autistic community as best I could. To prepare for the printing process, I have collected from the website, done some technical editing and adjusted wording to account for the fact that I used images on the website that I do not have permission to print. Essentially, you are getting the exact experience that was available on my blog. I am presenting these essays in the order published, as well. I've been advised that this may give some insight into me, in some way... but don't look too deep for that meaning.

001 – Introduction from the Website

EDIT: It has recently been pointed out to me that throughout this series, I use the word "We" when referring to Autism Spectrum Disorder (ASD) individuals. It has been argued that the use of this word in this manner can be interpreted as my speaking for everyone on the Autistic Spectrum. This has never been my intent. I use the word we as a general word. I do not presume to speak for everyone on the spectrum. I am only an expert on my own experiences, and cannot speak for anyone else. However, in my research and discussions with NTs, Aspies, and psychiatric professionals – I have been assured that I have a fundamental understanding of the mechanisms and underlying causes of the behaviors and issues associated with Asperger's and Autistic Spectrum Disorders. So, when I use the word "WE", I am only talking in a general sense.

This is the first part of my new series. As the title says, it is about the special care that Aspies need. Having an Aspie in your life is a bit like having a puppy. It will effect all aspects of your life. If you're not ready for this kind of time investment you may wish to steer clear and get a lizard or some other small animal that can be decorative.

However, if you feel you are ready for this, the following rules should help you out quite a bit.

1) Aspies need a great deal of privacy. While we, for the most part, want to be social – it is HARD for us. I know you've heard this before – and you will hear it a lot in this series – but what you do naturally, we have to work at. And frankly, there is a great deal of effort and anxiety in this for us. And by anxiety, I am referring to the clinical definition of Anxiety. So, respect your Aspie's need for privacy, whether it is shown as a desire to be

completely alone in his room or to simply hang out with you in the living room.

- Anxiety is a multisystem response to a perceived threat or danger. It reflects a combination of biochemical changes in the body, the patient's personal history and memory, and the social situation. As far as we know, anxiety is a uniquely human experience. Other animals clearly know fear, but human anxiety involves an ability, to use memory and imagination to move backward and forward in time, that animals do not appear to have. The anxiety that occurs in post traumatic syndromes indicates that human memory is a much more complicated mental function than animal memory. Moreover, a large portion of human anxiety is produced by anticipation of future events. Without a sense of personal continuity over time, people would not have the "raw materials" of anxiety.

2) NEVER, EVER, EVER embarrass them in public. This is not an admonition to avoid parent like behavior. Your Aspie will do things that are very odd by Neurotypical standards. Don't call your aspie out on it. This will add to his anxiety in ways that you cannot imagine. Your Aspie can't even imagine them either. At our core, we want, very desperately to fit in, and we need time to process things. If we are trying to process something we have messed up on, socially, we will be unable to continue other social interactions and it will exacerbate the problem. While this seems like a small problem, it will continue to cause more and more embarrassment in that situation, which will make your Aspie more and more uncomfortable until he won't feel comfortable going out into any similar social situations... ever.

3) New situations are scary for us. And by new situations, I

mean things that you take for granted. If NTs go to a bar regularly, it is very easy to go to another bar and enjoy themselves. A different bar for an Aspie is a completely different situation entirely. It is a new room, with new people, new sights, sounds, feel, and smells… So when you say, "Hey! Let's go to that new place! I hear it kicks ass!" Your Aspie will go along with you, but will need time. The previous example is just that… an example. Any little change makes it a new situation. So, in new situations, give them a few minutes to observe. Give them the time they need to work out the dynamics of what they are seeing. Let them wade in slowly.

4) When you ask your Aspie a question, they will need time to think about their answer. Unlike your average Neurotypical, we don't have instant reactions to questions. (IN MOST SITUATIONS). Sometimes, we will, but for the most part, we need time to reason out our responses. Give us that time to think. Don't demand an instant response. When forced into that situation, we will have problems. We want to please you, but we tend to deal in the absolutes of truth. So, when pressed to give an answer that we haven't reasoned out, you are pushing us into cognitive dissonance. Cognitive dissonance can be uncomfortable; over stimulating; and, in some cases, can actually cause mental damage. Further, the answer you get will most likely have nothing to do with our actual reasoning process, but will be something stated in an effort to please you and lessen our distress. Also, once we have a chance to finish our reasoning processes, the actual answer will be stated. If we can't think it out, there are often misunderstandings.

5) When at all possible, please avoid interrupting your Aspie. At times, we have difficulty communicating in a way that is understandable. To do it, we must organize

our thoughts before we speak. When we are interrupted, out train of thought is interrupted as well. Your Aspie will have to start from the beginning. We can't pick up in the middle and resume. Since our thoughts are very ordered – **A** to **B** and **B** to **C**, if we are interrupted at **D** on our way to **F**, we will have to start at a, to make sure we can get everything working again. Continued interruption, ESPECIALLY at the same point in the conversation can be exceedingly distressing. Further, we tend towards a model of low self esteem and interrupting us can tell us (*even if it's incorrect*) that what we have to say is of little worth and is not appreciated by the listener. This can be devastating to the Aspie ego. Keep in mind, if you're being spoken to by an Aspie more than a week after you met them, they have welcomed you into their circle, and as such, your opinion means a great deal more to them than it would be for a Neurotypical friend.

6) If you are expecting a change in your life, especially one that is likely to have ANY effect on an Aspie friend, give them advanced warning. And by any change, I mean *ANY* change. The brand of coffee at your house, the color of your uniform, your hat, the times of arrival and departure, foods in the house. Your Aspie can adapt READILY to any given situation, IF you give him time to adjust. Most of the time, this is as simple giving us a couple weeks of warning. We just need time to process the information. Keep in mind, sudden changes in environment (AND YOUR HAT IS PART OF THAT ENVIRONMENT – IT IS PART OF WHAT YOU ARE) are distressing. It changes the status quo and we have to adjust to it. Think about it this way – if you have a very small trickling stream of water and you drop a small stone into the water, it will disrupt the flow. At least, it will at first. Eventually, the small waves will settle and

the water will flow around the stone and into new channels. Our minds are a great deal like that. Give us time to establish a new flow.

7)   Give your Aspie a chance to finish what he's doing before changing activities. You might not see any activity going on, but we need time to make a bookmark, finish writing a sentence, get to a save point, arrange things in a pleasing manner… 15 minute warnings before it's time to go, or before dinner or any change in activity will make your life a great deal easier. A lack of warning can lead to oppositional behavior or outright melt downs.

8)   There is a time and place for everything. The time for teaching new skills and reprimands is in private – not at an event or surrounded by people. It is hard for us to comprehend that, after working as hard as we do to fit in and be like everyone else – we messed it up. And when you call us out on it, it causes cognitive dissonance and embarrassment. Embarrassment is much easier to deal with at home than it is at an event. We want to learn, we want to grow, but we need time to practice it and integrate it into our thought processes.

9)   Respect the fact that your Aspie doesn't need the same amount of socialization that a Neurotypical does. most NTs don't feel complete without a small circle of close friends a larger circle of friends and an even larger circle of acquaintances. Your Aspie doesn't need those, most of us need a small circle of friends. That's it. We need those rare few who "get it" and nothing more. Respect that. The best way to respect that is by not pressuring us to get out and make new friends. Feel free to introduce us to new people, but anticipate and respect the fact that 80% of the time, the person you introduce us to will

never make it past the acquaintance stage. Also anticipate and respect the fact that another 19% of the time, we probably won't like the person. There is 1% of the people in your life that we can become friends with, but for that to happen, the stars must align. The situation, temperament, mood and timing has to be just right for that person to gain the coveted status of "friend."

Whether or not you know it… or even if your aspie knows it… there are sensory issues associated with Asperger's Syndrome. In many cases, these are intrinsically intertwined with other conditions and issues... So much so that your aspie may not be aware that they have sensory issues. Also. There is a chance that they will have no sensory issues. But if they do – here's a run down for you.

There are five senses and each can be effected in a different manner…

Visual issues:

Often you can spot an aspie with visual issues by tendencies towards taking pleasure in visual things… Colors, art, photographs, movies… these can all be indications, but not sure signs. Visual issues can consist of any number of conditions. Your aspie might have problems with bright lights, darkness, too many colors… it might be sudden changes in light levels. Sometimes it will be a quality of the light (like the overheads in certain department stores), a riot of colors, or other things that the average NT won't be notice or experience.

Scent Issues:

Your aspie might have a highly developed sense of smell, allowing him to cook effectively without ever tasting the meal before serving it, or be able to track a specific smell through the store. The problem with that is that he will smell EVERYTHING. I mean EVERYTHING. Things you will not be able to smell he will smell extremely well… unpleasant smells can be a domineering assault. Scent issues can be confused with taste relatively easily, because 85% of taste is actually smell (look it up).

Auditory Issues:

As with all of the other senses, your aspie may have a finely tuned sense of hearing. Perfect pitch, relative pitch, a deep resonance with music or just sound in general are all symptoms. Auditory issues may manifest as problems with loud noises, issues with specific tones, issues with background noise, but sounds can be problematic for your aspie.

Taste Issues:

I don't think I know of any aspie that does not really have sort of issues with taste. We all tend to be really picky with what we will eat. You will find that, at times, it is difficult to get your Aspie the right nutrition. They will often obsess on one food for a long time… one aspie I knew would only eat strawberry pie and cheese for almost a year… For myself, it's often lasagna or pizza. Your aspie might not like certain flavors… and as you know, when and aspie dislikes something… he HATES it.

Touch Issues:

The extremely high strung nature of aspie senses can manifest in touch issues. It's hard to describe how these issues will manifest… but often, your aspie may not like being touched, find hugs and handshakes to be distasteful (at best) and may not want cuddling or sex at all. (Some aspies even find sex to be… "Icky"). It can also be an obsession with a specific type of cloth, hatred of clothing that is not very soft, or that is constricting in some way. It's difficult to tell. But I don't know of any of us that don't have some sort of issue with the sense of touch.

Often, your aspie will find themselves overwhelmed by sensory input… This can result in distasteful events. If you are out with your aspie and find him getting agitated, quiet or overly animated, your aspie may be suffering from over-stimulation. There are two main problems with this…

1) Your aspie is overhwelmed… and this can lead to severe irritation, aggressiveness and worse.

2) Your aspie might not even know that this is happening.

Failure to remove your aspie from the situation may result in a temper tantrum or even a melt down.

I won't go into the anatomy of a temper tantrum and meltdown in this issue… but if you see your aspie in distress, you may want to remove them from the situation. Unfortunately, this needs to be done in a tactful and delicate manner… In a way that avoids pointing out that your Aspie is having issues – as this can exacerbate your problems.

Just get him to a place he feels comfortable and wait for a while… the feeling of over-stimulation will fade and then everything will be fine.

03 – Aspies and Stress

It is common for people with Asperger's to be upset by little things throughout their day. It can happen quickly and relatively easily. Sometimes, the least little thing can set your Aspie off.

Aspies and ASD Individuals often suffer from stress from environmental influences that other people would either take in stride or not even notice. School issues, social issues, the texture of food, The texture or smell of their clothing.

Since OCD often accompanies Autistic Spectrum Disorders, Aspies can be overwhelmed by many simple things. Obsessive thoughts tumble around in our heads and cycle over and over and over. Little things like noise, scent, textures, disorder… can all interrupt an obsessive cycle. This can cause cognitive dissonance that can really only be resolved by going back to the compulsive behavior.

While cognitive dissonance is the basis of neurotypical decision processes, but your Aspie has a big problem dealing with it. Neurotypicals have a spectrum of likes and dislikes; (i,e, I like thing A more than thing B.) Aspies tend to have no subtlety in likes and dislikes – it is all or nothing. Your Aspie will say "I like it" or "I hate it." There will be no in between. This polarized mentality makes it difficult for your Aspie to get past the obsessive thoughts.

Obsessive thoughts
Once we're in that place, nothing matters is those obsessive thoughts. It brings us pleasure. The cognitive dissonance associated with interrupting the obsessive thoughts brings us psychological pain.

As a result, your Aspie will often be perceived as intolerant of their environment as well as other people. Anxiety will build in unstructured settings and situations where people are milling about. Noise in these situations can cause acute stress. Your Aspie may not be able to stand having people too close to them.

Every Aspie will be different, but mark my words, they will have their stress triggers. Younger Aspies may react to these with a temper tantrum, and older Aspies may have outbursts because things aren't going their way. These outbursts are not childish behavior, but a way to translate their distress into something that allows them to put it out of themselves… to get it away.

As much as it pains me to say it, you may, at times, just have to give in to your Aspies idiosyncratic behavior. This may mean quieting down the environment, or keeping items in specific places in orders. It definitely means that your Aspie will be dressing in clothing he or she feels comfortable in – and this can mean a very limited wardrobe selection. Learn to embrace it, or do the kind thing and get your Aspie into an environment where they are cherished as opposed to grudgingly accepted. Your Aspie may be about 13 degrees off cool, but they will not thrive any other way.

Also, lack of sleep is another major issue for your Aspie. The stress hormones associated with sleeplessness build up until rest can be achieved. However, the obsessive thoughts and compulsive behaviors may (actually will) interfere with a good night's sleep. Most Aspies don't want to take medication to sleep. (In fact, most Aspies rebel against the idea of taking any medications. We'll cover that more later.) Especially since the side effects of these medications can lead to unpleasant sensations, grogginess or worse.

Most Neurotypical stress reduction techniques simply don't work with the Aspie psyche. Be prepared for your Aspie to want

to have alone time, rigid rules or even a nap when stressed.
These things will help him relax, granting a sense of security.
And this will lead to a happier aspie.

04 – So... Your Aspie is Upset

The following part in the series is not intended as an accusatory statement towards anyone who might be reading this. This covers a lot of ground that you may have witnessed, or even done yourself. Don't take it personally – you honestly didn't know.

So… your Aspie is upset and you don't know why.

There is a good chance that someone said something that your Aspie felt was completely out of line or offensive… And while it is easy to do something that an Aspie finds offensive, there are some things that Neurotypicals will say or do that are… Well… just not right.

Some of these, I will try to explain WHY these things are offensive… Some, I will just let you try to suss it out on your own. Most of them, I will simply outline what we are not saying… What is going on in our head and not being spat at the offending NT.

1. **You're just using Asperger's/autistism as an excuse to be rude.**
    Why is this rude? Well… Think about it. Your Aspie has just been accused of being a liar, for one. Aspergians tend towards truth… to the cost of harmony and even friendship. So, the concept that we would lie about something that causes us such distress is so foreign that many Aspies will rebel at the thought, to the point of ACTUALLY being rude intentionally.

2. **I saw of The Big Bang Theory/Rain man/Sherlock/Bones/this episode of House/Adam/ Parenthood… So I know ALL about autism!**
    Right. We live it and even WE don't know all about it.

Even the experts on Autism don't know all about it. Nerotypicals often assume that they have expertise beyond their knowledge and then will immediately tell us how to deal with our own lives.

3. **Wait, are you ACTUALLY Autistic, or do you just have Asperger's?**
I don't need to tell you why this is offensive… If you cannot see why, you should probably read a different blog – you won't deal well here.

4. **Have you tried Swimming with Dolphins/riding horses/meds/hugs/special diets/chelation/not being autistic?**
Have you tried any of those things? Have you tried the "as seen on TV" diets or magnets? No? Why not?

5. **Is your parent/guardian/care taker here?**
I am an adult. As they say in Louisiana, "I am a grown ass man." I do have people that help me a great deal… but those people are not me… Just because I exist on the Autistic Spectrum does not mean that I need a babysitter.

6. **You seem so… Normal!**
I am normal, just not typical.

7. **What do you mean you don't want a hug?**
What do you mean, "What do you mean you don't want a hug?" I mean that I don't like being touched by people that I don't know and you are wanting me to engage in a relatively intimate act with someone that I don't know. Piss off.

8. **Quiet hands!**
Don't tell me what to do… I stim, not because I want to,

but because I have NO OTHER CHOICE… SO… quiet lips!

9. **But you have a job/go to school/have a social life… with people!**
Yes… because we are primates… Primates are social creatures. How dare you imply that we are not fit for public consumption.

10. **You don't mean "Autistic." You mean "has autism."**
Yes. I do mean Autistic. YOU exist outside the spectrum. We exist within it. How DARE YOU tell me what label I apply to myself?

11. **Labels go on soup cans. Not people.**
You know what labels are? They are words… symbols that allow us to communicate effectively. Without labels, we cannot describe our world. Wind, water, coffee, pizza, dogs, cats… These are labels. Learn to live with it.

12. **I don't think you have autism. You're so social/smart/pretty/nice/… You have feelings/I mean, I like you!**
No offense intended, but are you a psychiatric professional? No? Then, may I ask why you feel comfortable diagnosing, or in this case, offering a contrary diagnosis? Seriously? No… If you tell me that YOU don't think that I have a condition that I struggle with every day, I would really like to see your credentials and if you ARE qualified – please offer an alternative diagnosis… Even if you are, I would like to ask – why do you think that you can make a call like that in moments when diagnosis of any psychiatric condition takes days or months of experience with the patient?

13. **The cause of autism is geeks marrying geeks/flouride in the water/vaccines/too much TV/inflammation/stress/the internet/x-rays/yeast/vaccines/mercury!**
I promise you that we are far more up to date on this issue than the average person. They don't know what causes it. Period. You telling us what caused out condition is a bit like me coming into your office and telling you how to do your job.

14. **You're autistic? But I like you/there's nothing wrong with you/I never would have guessed/give me a hug. It's going to be okay/I'm so sorry/that is so sad.**
Yes. No. I don't want a hug. I know it will be okay. Piss off.

15. **You must be very high functioning.**
That is nice of you to say. I am sorry that you are such a mental deficient that you cannot understand that this is insulting and calls attention to our condition, and is NOT a compliment... Hey, moron, your bus is leaving.

16. **Why are you doing that? Stop it! People can see you!**
Why are you assaulting me with your words? Why are you constantly talking loudly and so fast when I am OBVIOUSLY suffering from anxiety and sensory issues in public. Thank you so very much for calling attention to something that is already embarrassing.

17. **Autistic people are so spiritual/refreshing/honest/real/close to god/authentic/nasty.**
No. We are not. We are people. We are no more or less of these things than any NT is. Making a blanket statement that elevates or insults us as a whole is just degrading... More so to you than to us... but still.

18. I read Temple Grandin's book!
Good for you. You do realize that there are many Aspies
and Autistic Spectrum individuals that have
accomplished as much, if nor more than Grandin, right?

19. So, what's it like being retarded?
I don't know. Why don't you tell me?

**20. I like Autistic people almost as much as I like real
people.**
(This one happened to me personally)… Real people?
You mean, as opposed to the mask wearing, constantly
telling little social lies, giving lip service to ideals they
don't actually stick to Neurotypical people? Those are
the real people you are talking about? I prefer the "fake"
autistics, thank you.

21. ***dumping toothpicks on the floor* Count these!**
First, what say you count the number of kicks to the
groin I am going to serve up.

22. Just get over it.
How about you come over the fence… try seeing it from
our standpoint… you blast us with noise, assault us with
color and light… and we're supposed to get over what
would amount to psychological torture of wartime
prisoners? How about you get over yourself?

23. Aren't we all just a little autistic?
No. We aren't. Because if EVERYONE was a little
autistic, we'd be switching places… if EVERYONE was
autistic, then autistic would be the mean, the standard or
the normal… making us the Neurotypicals… and what
is now considered normal would have the problem…

Now, what I have listed here are extreme examples… but there are little things that are said every day of my life that are part of the Neurotypical social regime that are offensive. We understand that you jockey for social standing constantly and have a need to slash and cut, and most of that doesn't even phase you… But, honestly, we aren't part of your social hierarchy. These words that are used in every day life can be anxiety inducing, stressful, hurtful and downright devastating to your Aspie…

Now, if you've been good to your Aspie and not been guilty of these things, congratulations. If you have witnessed someone else doing it to your Aspie and you didn't step in, you may find that the trust you worked so hard to earn from your Aspie may be damaged.

You may not know how these words hurt him… but he can't see how you didn't see it.

So, to ensure your Aspie's happiness and comfort, step in and help ameliorate any issues like this. You will be pleased by the results. And rest assured, your Aspie will come to your rescue when he perceives any injustice.

05 – Cognitive Dissonance, Decision Making and Communication

Cognitive dissonance is defined as the discomfort experienced when simultaneously holding two or more conflicting cognitions: ideas, beliefs, values or emotional reactions.

In a state of dissonance, people may sometimes feel "disequilibrium": frustration, hunger, dread, guilt, anger, embarrassment, anxiety, etc.

After reading those two statements, you are asking yourself, "What is cognitive dissonance, really?"

The best example of cognitive dissonance I can come up with is this: Have you ever been at the table at a restaurant, reached for your glass, but instead of coca-cola you take a big swig of sprite instead. (insert your favorite beverage, don't nitpick this part of it, please). That moment where your brain screams out "What the hell, man? What? Where? Why? What???" That is cognitive dissonance.

In its gentler forms, cognitive dissonance is intrinsic to the Neurotypical decision making process. In an decision making process (which is every moment of every day) Neurotypical brains pits its wants against one another. (In this example, needs are extreme wants).

I want to be in shape, but I want an ice cream cone more.
I want to eat healthy, but I want McDonald's more.
I want cigarettes, but I don't want to die from them.

Each of these examples is simplified, but it gets the point across. Two different cognitions are pitted against one another. The levels of wantiness are compared and the choice that is wanted more is the one that is decided on.

These wants can be enhanced by many factors – addiction, association, habit, etc.

The mechanisms are much the same in an Aspie as they are in an NT, but certain differences in wiring and cognition lead to a drastically different outcome.

In your relationship with your Aspie, it will be rare that you will come across something that your Aspie "kind of likes". Aspies tend to be all or nothing… translation: your Aspie will (as a general rule) LOVE something; or they will HATE it. The only things, thoughts or ideas your Aspie will feel moderately about are things they have no information on or have never experienced.

This makes decision making difficult at times. If your Aspie has video games as one of their SPECIAL interests, they will be able to rattle off a long list of games that they have a palpable and overriding desire to own or play. If you buy them one of these games, they will be infinitely prolific in their thanks.

Now… Take your Aspie to Game Stop, Play-n-trade, or Best Buy with a gift card that has enough money on it for one of these games. I recommend bringing a folding chair, a drink and something to eat – you are in for a long wait.

Where an NT would walk in and say to themselves, "I have the money for one game… the one I want the MOST" or "the one I have been waiting for the longest is…" – your Aspie can't do that.

When your Aspie likes or wants something, it is at 100%. There is no, "I have interest in that game," or "I kinda want to play that game"… There is only, "I WANT THAT GAME."

In this example, the NT has values ranging from 0-100 of interest… Game A is at 10%, Game B is at 89% and Game C is at 45%. The NT will pick Game B because his interest i that game is higher.

Meanwhile, the Aspie has three settings -1 for I hate it, 0 for I don't know it, and 1 for I LOVE IT. So Game A is at 1, Game B is at 1 and Game C is at 1. I am sure you can see how the conflict resolution is difficult in this situation.

And this is how your Aspie will live his life, constantly trying to resolve the dissonance caused by equal wants and needs.

How does this relate to communication? I am glad you asked.

Since there are no shades of gray (grays are defined by a percentage from 0% – white, to 99%- almost black), your Aspie will apply the same cognitions and functionality to words and communication. There are several ways that this will apply to communication.

The first way is that they will use the dictionary definitions (or what they think the definitions are) without the emotional connotations often attached to the words. Example: Prostitute versus Whore. These two words are identical in meaning. A person that performs sexual favors in exchange for money, goods or services.

Yet, when dealing with a prostitute, it is offensive to call them a whore. While the words have the same definitions, they do not mean the same thing. Your Aspie will not know this, and will be bewildered by the fact that this person is offended by being labeled in a way that the Aspie feels is accurate. This will lead to a bout of cognitive dissonance.

Why? Because in this moment, your Aspie is confronted with the fact that his perception of the world is wrong – something that we battle with every day. When you spend most of your life trying to understand and be understood (which is a lifelong and constant battle for Aspies), being slapped in the face with the fact that you failed at it is demoralizing.

The cognitions at work are simple. "I've got this. I understand it." versus "Wait! What?" The conflicting thoughts resonate in a dissonant manner. The Aspie brain is unable to let go of the thoughts and move on…

The second way is lies. Your Aspie won't lie. Let me reword that… There are some Aspies that have problems with telling the truth… there are comorbid issues that can cause this, but we are discussing your average, run of the mill Aspie. (as if there is such a thing) If your Aspie lies, there is something really big at work here and is something that you need to sit him down and discuss.

But your average Aspie is confounded by lies. Neurotypicals lie at every turn. Most of them are harmless little social lies. They will compliment each others clothes, lie about their feelings, wear emotional masks and say things like, "I'm fine."

Your Aspie will take all these words at face value. When you had a deeper meaning behind what you said, your Aspie will not catch it. As a result, most NTs get upset and the Aspie is bewildered… Confusion results and cognitive dissonance follows.

From the Aspie standpoint, Neurotypical conversation is fraught with these potholes – little lies, illogical behavior and outright irrational communication patterns… Any and all of these can cause a dissonant episode for your Aspie.

Cognitive dissonance for the average NT is something that is easily dealt with. As with the soda example, the dissonant episode will last for a short time, then the NT mind is able to shake it off (in this example, almost literally). They shake their head and walk away, mentally speaking, from the cognitively dissonant episode with ease. Neurotypicals evolved like this to prevent damage, it is just how you are.

In your Aspie, a dissonant episode is a great deal harder to walk away from. Cognitive Dissonance can actually remain in the Aspie mind for a long time, and if it is strong enough, it can cause damage. Actual, physical damage to the Aspie brain.

Interrupting the cognitive dissonance loop can be done easily by distracting your Aspie. This can be done with absurdity, a special interest, a favored treat, a change of topic or a change of location. Remembering this can be a required skill for the happiness of your Aspie.

06 – Some Advice for Parents of Young Austics

My friend (and I do consider you a friend) Jon suggested this issue of "Care and Feeding." At first I was resistant. I felt that my childhood was lacking in anything that could be helpful to parents of Autistics. I was raised by religious fundamentalists that felt that what was wrong with me could be solved by nothing more than prayer. Couple that with multiple head traumas, the memory loss associated with severe bipolar disorder and the memory loss from medications from treatment of same… Honestly, I really don't remember much of my childhood that could be described as anything other than mental and physical abuse.

Then I thought about it. I mean, I really thought about it and came up with some advice that I believe would have helped my family when I was growing up. Since I have no frame of reference, I can only give the advice that I can extrapolate from my own personal experiences. Hopefully, this will be helpful to any reading this…

If something seems wrong with your child, do not ignore it.

My parents thought that the referrals and comments from teachers and other professionals as reactionary. As such, they were unwilling to see that I needed help. They felt that I was just a problem child. At their core, all children – NT and Autistic Spectrum alike want to be accepted, respected and loved. If a child is misbehaving, or seems to be oppositional, there is a reason. Do not let the stigma against mental illness in our culture color your perceptions and cause more harm to your child than good.

Learn all that you can about autism.

As of today's count, about 1 in 68 children has been diagnosed with an Autism Spectrum Disorder (which includes

Asperger's Syndrome). While I believe that ASD is an over-used diagnosis, the fact remains that there are a large number of Autistic diagnoses.

Autism is not contagious. At this point, there is a great deal of speculation as to what causes it, but NO ONE knows what causes it. I can state with almost 100% surety, that it is not yeast, geeks marrying geeks, vaccines, mercury, fluoride in the water or almost any other theory that is out there. You can't "catch" it. You either have it or you don't. And if you have it, you've had it since before you were born.

Autism Spectrum Disorders are developmental disabilities that will impact a child's social skills, communication skills and behavior. Most often, Autism is going to be diagnosed during the formative years. What this means is that you need to work with them because diagnosis, treatment and skill training the only way to help a child with autism reach their potential.

It cannot be treated. Medications can help with the symptoms, but that is all. They will not help the child's condition. THIS IS NOT TO SAY THAT YOUR CHILD SHOULD NOT BE MEDICATED – IF YOUR MENTAL HEALTH PROFESSIONAL STATES THAT IT IS THEIR PROFESSIONAL OPINION THAT THE CHILD BE MEDICATED, TAKE THAT ADVICE UNDER SERIOUS ADVISEMENT. However, the principle purpose and goal of treatment for Autistic Spectrum individuals is to improve their quality of life and their overall ability to function.

Talk to your doctor and read, read, read on the subject.

It will be a journey – there is no ONE solution or treatment/education regimen.
Autism Spectrum behaviors WILL change with time. As the child develops and certain areas of the brain become active and

develop, their understanding and processing of certain stimuli will change. Another reason for this is the development of coping and functional skill sets being applied.

While children with Autism respond (on the whole) best to a highly structured and specialized environment, what is often forgotten is that that structure must evolve with the child. As such, the treatment plan must be re-evaluated as often as is needed…

Sometimes, this can mean that a treatment plan will be in place for months or years and then suddenly need to be changed. Other times, this means that a treatment plan will need to be updated on a weekly basis.

Your child is VERY sensitive to changes in body chemistry, texture, light, sound, taste, and especially the changes caused by medications.
With the high incidents of sensory issues involved with Autistic Spectrum individuals, this can be problematic. (Please reference this entry Aspies and sensory issues for more information) This means that your Autistic child may become oppositional to a situation, food, clothing, medicine or simply the sensations associated with physical maturity. As a parent, it is your responsibility to watch for the telltale signs of a sensory issue. I wish I could tell you what to look for, but each Autistic Spectrum individual's "tells" are different – one thing to watch for is stimming. If your Autistic child stims – it is a sure sign that something is wrong.

A strong social network can be your greatest asset.
Any chronic illness in the family can be an emotional and trying situation. The day-to-day care of Autistic Spectrum individuals can be extremely stressful. A lot of this stress comes from the lack of social and communication skills of the Autistic Spectrum individual and their inability to express their thoughts

and feelings adequately.

Further, making sure your child gets the care and treatment that is needed can be a challenge – especially due to the lack of social services and support infrastructure. Add to this the worries about diagnoses, prognosis and well being, the situation can become almost untenable.

A strong social support network can help you out with emotional issues – someone who is a confidant and who will help you survive the failures and rejoice in your victories; Institutional – doctors, teachers, caregivers, therapists that are there to provide information and professional advice; and practical support – neighbors, family members and friends that you can rely on to help you out in an emergency.

Teach your FAMILY about autism.
Teach your family about your child's condition. By family, I mean ALL of the family members that will have contact with you child. It is all too easy for a family member who is ignorant of your Autistic child's needs can cause mental trauma and cognitive dissonance. Many people will consider this to be an embarrassing thing to talk about. Think about the embarrassment that would be caused by a tantrum or meltdown that could easily have been avoided by a little information.

USE CAUTION when considering unproven treatment methods.
As a parent, you want to do what is best for your child. Often, this will mean grasping at ANY proffered cure.

There are many unproven therapies used to treat autism. The safety and effectiveness of these is not known. These therapies and treatments circulate through conspiracy websites, uninformed word of mouth and ignorant media. These treatment options have not bee subjected to scientific study and therefore the validity and safety of the treatment cannot be assured. Even if a friend had a fantastic success using the method suggested, there is no guaranty that it will work for you, or even if it is the treatment that was a result of the treatment in question.

Be cautious of a treatment suggestion if the treatment:

- is based on simplified theories
- promises dramatic results
- sounds too good to be true
- benefits more than a single condition
- is based on anecdotal evidence with no scientific backing
- there are no risks or side effects, therefore no studies are needed
- claims it can CURE autism
- can only be found on websites with no citations. If you cannot track the information, **it is wrong.**

Some of the unproven therapies are: (the following information was harvested from various sources, including Wikipedia)
- a macrobiotic diet. This is predicated on a belief that abnormal yeast colonization is the cause of Autism. Jenny McCarthy claims that her son was Autistic, but a macrobiotic diet cured him. Her son never had Autism.
- Auditory integration training (AIT). Based upon a theory that autism is caused by hearing problems that result in distorted sounds or over-sensitivity to noises, this treatment delivers music through special devices.
- Facilitated communication. This method uses a keyboard to assist communication. It has not been found to be helpful and in some cases has been harmful.
- Secretin. This treatment uses an IV injection of secretin (a hormone that stimulates the pancreas and liver) to

manage autistic behavior. Anecdotal reports have shown improvement in autism symptoms, including sleep patterns, eye contact, language skills, and alertness. Several clinical trials conducted in the last few years have found no significant improvements in symptoms between children with autism who received secretin and those who received a placebo.

- Chelationtherapy. Mercury exposure as a cause of autism is the basis for this therapy, which uses medications to help the body eliminate the toxins. Children with autism often have a craving for nonfood items or unusual diets that may result in mercury exposure; therefore, mercury exposure may be more of an effect of autism than a cause.
- Immune globulin therapy. An intravenous (IV) injection of immune globulin is based on the assumption that autism is caused by an autoimmune abnormality.

Take time for relaxation.

The best tool you have in your arsenal for dealing with the rigors and difficulties of living with an autistic spectrum child is spending time with them. Take time and schedule downtime… quiet time… not only will your Autistic Child feel more accepted… you will learn more about them and you will alleviate a lot of the problems associated with stress issues and over stimulation.

07 – Tantrum Avoidance

In past entries in this series, I have covered possible causes of agitation in your Aspie, but I have yet to talk about diffusing the situation. Management of stress, agitation and anger issues is an art form. While art is not something that is for everyone, but mastering this art can benefit you a great deal. It can benefit your Aspie even more.

What most Mental Health professionals neglect to tell people (or are, perhaps, ignorant of it) is that tantrums, anger outbursts and meltdowns are as hard, if not harder on your Aspie (and in fact, all Autistic Spectrum individuals). We don't want to be angry, loud, hateful or obnoxious and when we breakdown outside of our own paradigm of thought, we are inflicted with cognitive dissonance. As we have discussed previously, cognitive dissonance is uncomfortable at best… and can cause damage to your Aspie's psyche at it's worst.

Please watch this video before you continue reading: http://vimeo.com/14409696. I wanted you to watch that video so that you could understand what a profound event a meltdown can be.

So, when you notice that your Aspie is starting to become agitated, try the following steps…

Safety First
If your Aspie has become physically violent, thrashing about or flailing – (This can happen LONG before a tantrum actually starts.) remember safety first… DO NOT attempt to restrain them. This can lead to you getting injured and then you won't be able to help your Aspie. FURTHER, it can accelerate the process and jump them straight into a full blown meltdown. Instead, remove any objects that can be damaging, knocked over or may fall, causing injury.

Communicate

If your Aspie is still verbal, asking them what is causing the anxiety or stress can help identify a possible solution. This should be done in a respectful manner. Asking and Autistic Spectrum individual something like "What now?" will only exacerbate the problem and will accelerate the tantrum/melt down cycle.

Attempt to rectify the situation – post haste

If it is something that can be removed from the environment, remove it immediately (turn off the music or television, ask someone to leave the room, take away the abhorrent food item. If the cause cannot be removed, then relocate your Aspie to another location.

Limit Stimuli

If your Aspie has gone non-verbal, remove sources of stimulation. This means turn off the television, radio, music… if you can, turn down the lights. As we have discussed, Autistic Spectrum individuals often have problems with sensory input… We hear, feel, and see things a lot more potently than others. If your Aspie is non-verbal, they won't be able to tell you what is wrong. You have to try to anticipate the issues.

Physically calm your Aspie

THIS NEXT SUGGESTION IS ONLY FOR THOSE AUTISTIC SPECTRUM INDIVIDUALS THAT RESPOND WELL TO TOUCH FROM A FAMILIAR PERSON – DO NOT FORCE TOUCH ON YOUR ASPIE IF THEY ARE NOT KNOWN TO RESPOND TO IT FAVORABLY. It has been shown that some Autistic Spectrum individuals respond well and benefit from massage therapy. If your Aspie is one that responds to this, rubbing shoulders, head or back can have a rapidly soothing effect. My sister responds especially well to having someone stand behind her, place an arm across her shoulders and leaning your cheek on her head.

Help Them

Be observant… If they are agitated and have started tugging
at a piece of clothing, seem averse to a specific object, person,
etc. Help them. Help them remove the clothing. Help them by
asking the person to leave until the incident is over. Help them
by removing the offending object.

Speak in Soothing Tones

As we have discussed, your Aspie often suffers from being
hyper-vigilant. This means that your tone will be magnified in
their ears. If you are angry, they will become defensive on top
of everything else. And I mean it… be soothing… do not
condescend. Just because your Aspie is socially inept and is
having an issue that makes them seem child-like, condescension
will only worsen the issues.

Stay Calm

The calmer you are, the more likely you are to be able to
calm them down. If you panic – it is almost a sure bet that they
will, too.

Stay with Them

If this is scary for you, imagine how it is for them. We don't
want to be like this. We don't want to have tantrums and
meltdowns. These events are beyond our control, and are often
contrary to how we feel at the time. So our brain is betraying us.
Stay with your Aspie. If you leave – you are likely to add
anxiety or all out panic to the issue.

Sometimes, You Have to Let It Happen

Sometimes, it is inevitable – It will happen. This is not a
failure as a parent or guardian. It is just the way it is. If you
cannot manage the tantrum and eliminate it… You will have to
ride it out. Stay calm and keep your Aspie safe. Above all

else… DO NOT TAKE IT PERSONALLY. If your Aspie does not go non-verbal, they will likely say something hurtful that they do not mean. Seriously, don't take it personally… That is the tantrum speaking… Not the Aspie.

08 – Autism… It IS a disease.

Autistic Spectrum individuals and Parents/Family members of Autistic Spectrum individuals tend to rankle at the following statement.

Autism is a disease.

I find it odd that a group of people who are noted for their literal nature would react with such vehemence to such a simple statement.

The medical definition of a disease is *"an impairment of the normal state of the living animal or plant body or one of its parts that interrupts or modifies the performance of the vital functions, is typically manifested by distinguishing signs and symptoms, and is a response to environmental factors (as malnutrition, industrial hazards, or climate), to specific infective agents (as worms, bacteria, or viruses), to inherent defects of the organism (as genetic anomalies), or to combinations of these factors."*

For some reason, the word disease carries a stigma with it. There are negative connotations that Autistic Spectrum individuals and their families apply to the word. I don't understand it… and in most cases, the individuals getting offended with the application of the word. So, let's take a look at some of the arguments.

Autism isn't a disease because:
It occurs in both disabling and non-disabling forms.
Whether or not it is a disabling condition is not part of the definition of disease, nor should it be. Vitiligo, eczema, psoriasis, diabetes and lichen simplex chronicus are all diseases. Each of these are also non-disabling conditions. They are no less diseases because of that.

Autism is a disorder – autism isn't an illness.
Technically… it is an illness. The World English Dictionary defines an illness as "a disease or indisposition." Again, I will go back to the definition of a disease… "an impairment of the normal state of the living animal… that interrupts or modifies the performance of the vital functions." So, this argument is belied by the definition of disease.

It just means the brain is wired differently – not better or worse just… differently.
Wired Differently
This is the part of the definition of disease that states "that interrupts or modifies the performance of the vital functions, is typically manifested by distinguishing signs and symptoms." The fact that Autism Spectrum disorders have a set of symptoms fits into the distinguishing signs and symptoms. This argument typically comes from family. Speaking as an Autistic Spectrum individual… it is worse… over stimulation, stimming, meltdowns, tantrums, excessive cognitive dissonance and comorbid conditions make it worse.

Some people insist on labeling autism in a negative light.
I have made this point before, but there are often emotional connotations placed on words that have nothing to do with their actual definitions. I have often cited the words whore and prostitute. They both mean a person who has sex for money. Whore has an emotional impact that prostitute does not. If you call a prostitute a whore… they will become angry, often to the point of becoming enraged.

Obviously, the word disease has negative connotations that are not inherent to the word. Applying these connotations to a word defeats the purpose of having a dictionary.

Autism is not a disease – it can't be cured.

Again, nowhere in the definition does it mention that a disease can be cured. Diabetes is a disease. Lupus is a disease. Marfam's is a disease. None of these conditions can be can be cured. Therefore, curability is not a deciding factor as to whether or not it is a disease.

It is a syndrome, not a disease.
The dictionary defines a Syndrome as a "group of symptoms that together are characteristic of a specific disorder, disease, or the like." Look at that definition… I mean read it… A syndrome… is a group of symptoms that define a DISEASE… Just for the heck of it… the definition of symptom is " a phenomenon that arises from and accompanies a particular disease or disorder and serves as an indication of it."

"No… THIS is syndrome… He might be autistic… but… well… you get the point."

It goes on like that. The issues are that there is a lack of education and a surplus of emotion surrounding the word Disease.

As an Autistic Spectrum individual, I am forced to look at it from an objective standpoint. We either admit that there is something wrong with us… (and by wrong, I am referring to the fact that our mental and emotional functions are different… we are not normal, by the medical and psychological definitions of normal) – or – we accept what we are and move forward.

We have to decide.

The thing is – Autistic Spectrum Disorders have a set of symptoms. It can be diagnosed. There is research into diagnostic criteria and treatment plans.

If Autism isn't a disease, then we have no rights to mental

health treatment. We can't be disabled because of it. We can't expect the world to work with us. If we're just different, we have no right to tell people about our condition.

If we let the negative connotation of the word interfere; if we let our pride get in the way; we lose our greatest tool in the battle of Autistic Spectrum survival.

If you give up those tools, the Neurotypicals of the world are proven right. If there is nothing wrong with us… then we are just using it as an excuse to be rude; quiet hands are a necessity; we're probably just mentally retarded; we can just get over it; we are just anti-social; we are just attention seeking; there's no such thing as a special needs adult.

The mantra of "There is nothing wrong with me." is essential for the self esteem needed to function in NT society, but it is detrimental to our cause – which should be finding treatment plans and skill training that can help us survive the minefield of the NT world around us. If there is nothing wrong with us, we are (to the last of us) destined to end up miserable and alone. Our friends and family accept us… we should do ourselves the same courtesy.

This is what the NTs will see if we continue on the course set by "*Autism is not a disease!*"

I am drawing a line in the sand – swallow your pride like I have had to do, and accept it. A wise man I once knew said, "There is no forward motion without a backward notion." We can't know where we're going if we don't know where we have been.

The other option is to toe up to the line and stick our heads in the sand.

09 – Comorbidity and Your Aspie

Aspies are, on the best of days, considered weird by NTs. A lot of that is just the Asperger's, but at other times, it might be something else. Autistic Spectrum Disorders have a high incidence of comorbid conditions.

What does this mean? Well, comobidity is either the presence of one or more disorders (or diseases) in addition to a primary disease or disorder, or the effect of such additional disorders or diseases.

What does this mean for you? It means that your Aspie is an Autistic Spectrum individual, but in all likelihood, will have other mental health issues. It means that your Aspie may have other problems that will exacerbate the problems already associated with Asperger's Syndrome.

The following conditions are common amongst Autistic Spectrum individuals. These are things to watch out for. While your Aspie's Mental health professional may not

Anxiety Disorders

In spite of a lack of hard data, Anxiety Disorders are a common problem for Autistic Spectrum individuals. Most anxiety disorders aren't diagnosed in Autistic Spectrum individuals. The reason for this is that the symptomology of Anxiety Disorders overlaps and can be explained by the Autism diagnosis itself. Anxiety Disorders may be indicated by some or all of the following symptoms:

- Feelings of panic, fear, and uneasiness
- Uncontrollable, obsessive thoughts
- Repeated thoughts or flashbacks of traumatic experiences
- Nightmares
- Ritualistic behaviors, such as repeated hand washing

- Problems sleeping
- Cold or sweaty hands and/or feet
- Shortness of breath
- Palpitations
- An inability to be still and calm
- Dry mouth
- Numbness or tingling in the hands or feet
- Nausea
- Muscle tension
- Dizziness

Anxiety Disorders have been reported to occur in between 11% and 84% of Autism Spectrum individuals. The wide range in this case is due to differences in methodology of studies.

Bipolar Disorder

Manic Depression, or Bipolar Disorder, is considered a controversial diagnosis. It is often claimed to be comorbid with a plethora of other conditions. Due to the fact that Autism can display symptoms shared with mood and anxiety disorders, a bipolar diagnosis for an Autistic Spectrum individual may be difficult to attain. Worse yet, your Aspie may have been diagnosed as bipolar rather than being on the spectrum.

Manic Phase Symptoms

- Euphoria
- Inflated self-esteem
- Poor judgment
- Rapid speech
- Racing thoughts
- Aggressive behavior
- Agitation or irritation
- Increased physical activity
- Risky behavior
- Spending sprees or unwise financial choices

- Increased drive to perform or achieve goals
- Increased sex drive
- Decreased need for sleep
- Easily distracted
- Careless or dangerous use of drugs or alcohol
- Frequent absences from work or school
- Delusions or a break from reality (psychosis)
- Poor performance at work or school

Depressive Phase Symptoms
- Sadness
- Hopelessness
- Suicidal thoughts or behavior
- Anxiety
- Guilt
- Sleep problems
- Low appetite or increased appetite
- Fatigue
- Loss of interest in activities once considered enjoyable
- Problems concentrating
- Irritability
- Chronic pain without a known cause
- Frequent absences from work or school
- Poor performance at work or school

Further, according to the Mayo Clinic, there are other considerations when dealing with Bipolar disorders.

Seasonal changes in mood. As with seasonal affective disorder (SAD), some people with bipolar disorder have moods that change with the seasons. Some people become manic or hypomanic in the spring or summer and then become depressed in the fall or winter. For other people, this cycle is reversed — they become depressed in the spring or summer and manic or hypomanic in the fall or winter

Rapid cycling bipolar disorder. Some people with bipolar disorder have rapid mood shifts. This is defined as having four or more mood swings within a single year. However, in some people mood shifts occur much more quickly, sometimes within just hours.

Psychosis. Severe episodes of either mania or depression may result in psychosis, a detachment from reality. Symptoms of psychosis may include false but strongly held beliefs (delusions) and hearing or seeing things that aren't there (hallucinations).

Gastrointestinal Issues

Studies have described autistic enterocolitis – claiming that 50% of autistic children will experience persistent GI-tract problems. These can be anything from mild discomfort to moderate GI inflammation in both upper and lower intestinal tracts. There is lack of rigorous and published data to support these assertion, but anecdotal evidence by parents and Autistic Spectrum adults alike reveals that there is need for further study and research into this.

ADHD

I have already covered ADHD on my blog. The DSM-iv has prohibited certain co-diagnoses. One of those prohibitions is Autism Spectrum Disorders and Attention-Deficit Hyperactivity Disorder. HOWEVER, clinically significant symptoms of these conditions commonly occur. While the symptomology may be the same, in this case the causality may be different as children with both sets of symptoms will often not respond well to traditional ADHD treatments and may require a specialized treatment plan.

Mental retardation

In 2006, polls found that there was a common assumption that Autistic Spectrum individuals are mentally retarded. In reality, a 2001 study in Britain reported normal intelligence in 94% of Autistic children. This may be the case with Autistic Spectrum individuals, but it is different with Aspies. By definition, a diagnosis of Asperger's EXCLUDES the presence of Mental Retardation. If your Aspie is diagnosed with mental retardation AND Asperger's Syndrome, you need to find a NEW primary mental health care provider, as these two conditions are mutually exclusive.

Motor clumsiness

Children with Autistic Spectrum Disorders and Asperger's are commonly delayed in acquiring skills that require motor dexterity. This can effect every day functioning and they may appear physically awkward and "uncomfortable in their own skin." These difficulties can manifest in poor coordination, odd gait or posture, poor handwriting… it may go on to cause difficulties in visual-motor integration, visual-perceptual skills and conceptual learning. According to the Mayo Clinic ASD may show problems with proprioception (sensation of body position) on measures of apraxia (motor planning disorder), balance, tandem gait, and finger-thumb apposition.

Obsessive-compulsive disorder

Obsessive-compulsive disorder is characterized by recurrent obsessional thoughts or compulsive acts.

Obsessional thoughts are ideas, images or impulses that enter the individual's mind again and again in a stereotyped form. Obsessive thoughts cause distress because they are violent, obscene or are perceived as senseless or intrusive. Often, an OCD sufferer will try, most often unsuccessfully, to resist these thoughts. Unlike other conditions, these thoughts are recognized as the individual's own, but are problematic as they come unbidden and can be repugnant. OCD is not often diagnosed in conjunction with Autistic Spectrum disorders due to the obsessive tendencies associated with ASD. The main differences are that the rituals and obsessive interests of your

Aspie bring him pleasure and OCD sufferers can only hope for relief from the pressure of the obsession.

Tourette's syndrome

Some studies place the incident's of Tourrette's syndrome with ASD at 6.5% which is higher than the 2-3% prevalence of the condition in the general population. Several theories have been extended for this – common genetic factors, dopamine, glutamate or serotonin abnormalities.

Seizures

Autistic Spectrum Disorders often go hand in hand with Epilepsy. The risk factors change with age, cognitive level and language disorders. One out of four autistic children will develop a seizure disorder – often starting early in childhood and adolescence. Seizures are caused by abnormal electrical activity in the brain. These can cause a temporary loss of consciousness, convulsions, unusual movements or staring. Lack of sleep or high fever can be a contributing factor.

Tuberous sclerosis

Tuberous sclerosis – a genetic disorder that causes benign tumors to grow on vital organs and in the brain. This disease has a consistent association with the Autistic Spectrum. According to studies 1-4% of Autistic Spectrum individuals are diagnosed with Tuberous sclerosis. On the flip side 25-61% of individuals diagnosed with Tuberous sclerosis are on the spectrum.

This was, by no means, a comprehensive list, but these are – by far – the most common.

Research is one of your most important tools when dealing with comorbid conditions. If you notice behavior beyond the ken of standard Asperger's or Autistic Spectrum behavior – do your due diligence and seek additional diagnostics. If you are given a negative response, you are within your rights to seek a second or third opinion.

That being said – if you are given a negative on diagnosis several times… it may be a fact that your Aspie does not have the comorbid condition in question and may just be demonstrating their particular version of typical Aspie behavior…

Today someone pointed out something about this ongoing series. He said, "Don't you think that it's a bit ironic that you have a series called, 'Care and Feeding' and you haven't covered food issues, yet?" I pointed out that it was really odd that I hadn't covered it yet, but this was far from the definition of irony. He then set his head on fire and then stuck it in the garbage disposal to stop the pain. From what I understand, this is a common reaction to Neurotypical and Aspergian interactions.

Honestly, I am not really sure about that last part, but I wouldn't be surprised… and it would explain a lot. I mean, that is a common reaction to speaking with me.

So… here it is…

It doesn't matter what comorbid conditions, communication issues or sensory issues your Aspie has – it is likely that your Aspie will most likely have some kind of issues with food. The main reasons are Habits, Oppositional Behavior, Texture and Taste.

Habit

Asperger's Syndrome specifically, and Autistic Spectrum Disorders in general, have rituals listed as one of the diagnostic criteria. Many people take this to mean watching Judge Wopner and Jeopardy, having to do meaningless things ad infinitum, but this is not always the case. In many cases, you will find that your Aspie will fixate on one type or a very small subset of foods. This, believe it or not, can be a direct result of ritualistic behavior.

Sometimes, we get stuck. I knew an Aspie who was stuck on strawberry pie and cheese. That is all he would eat. When we are stuck in a food groove, it's may not even be a case of what we want. Obsessions work like that… we are literally stuck.

I know it's frustrating for the Neuotypicals in our lives, but imagine how hard it can be on your Aspie. Imagine if your Aspie is one of those few of us that cherish new experiences… Now imagine that he's stuck on crappy frozen pizzas, lasagna or french fries. Many of us buck against our obsessive tendencies. It is a sign of weakness… we can't even control our own brains.

Often, in these situations, you will find that trying to break the ritual will only lead to:

Oppositional Behavior

The phrase Oppositional Behavior is most often used when dealing with children and Oppositional Defiance Disorder. I, personally, feel that this should be considered a possible comorbid condition, but there have not been any studies linking ODD to Autistic Spectrum Disorders… And this, in my opinion, is only because it has not been looked for.

Oppositional Behavior is extreme disobedience. While experiencing an oppositional episode, you will see disobedience, unreasoning anger, possible LONG tantrums or even the dreaded MELTDOWN, often over trivial matters. It can lead to irrational arguments in which your Aspie will just not give up. Winning the argument will seem to be the most important thing at that moment. The odd thing is that during these episodes, the Aspie will not perceive themselves as being argumentative or even difficult.

Oppositional behavior is almost exclusively directed at an authority figure (parents, coach, or teacher. This can also lead to your Aspie being a mental bully, using language skills to taunt and abuse others.

Why is this listed under food issues? Well… Because often, new foods are often presented in a "Here – eat this" manner. Many times we don't like being TOLD what to do. If you have experience with and expect your Aspie to be oppositional, then you might want to try a "Would you like to try some of mine?" approach. Forcing your Aspie to eat a certain food against their will, will often lead to them deciding that they hate the dish, the genre, and the ingredients – and eventually COMPLETELY removing a large selection of foods from possible future meals.

Texture
I covered texture a LITTLE BIT in the sensory issues part of this series, but I feel that it could be expanded upon more.

Due to the fact that we are "Mis-wired", it is relatively easy for us to forge negative associations with any number of things. Anything that is new, unusual or uncertain can cause cognitive dissonance, stress and anxiety… Once one of those things has been triggered, there is little that can be done to go back.

Some Aspies will not eat spaghetti because it reminds them of worms. Some dislike Asian food because rice noodles are slimy, or don't taste right (because it's not wheat). Others hate okra because their first taste of if was cooked by someone who didn't know how and turned it into vegetable snot.

These texture issues may not even be something that your Aspie is aware of, and as such, they may not be able to even tell you WHY they don't like it.

Taste
Autistic Spectrum individuals tend to be hypersensitive. This is not about your Aspie's emotional state, but their perceptions. Hyper-sensitivity means that one or more of your Aspie's senses are far more acute than those of Neurotypical's.

When it comes to food, smell and taste can REALLY cause problems. Many people love the taste of red peppers, green peppers, sweet peppers and banana peppers, but I don't. The phytonutrients that give them a slightly bitter taste are… well… unbearably bitter for me. So much so that chicken cooked WITH peppers, whether or not I eat the pepper itself, is RUINED.

Spices can be overwhelming, as can acidic flavors, bitter ones, sweets, savory ones.

ANY overwhelming sensory input can cause stress, anxiety and cognitive dissonance. Once traumatized in this manner, it is a sure bet that your Aspie won't like the item in question.

How do I deal with food issues? I am afraid my Aspie is going to become malnourished or worse!

You will lose this fight.

First off… NEVER force your Aspie to eat something… that is a fight that you are GUARANTEED to lose. There are ways… often asking them if they want to try something, or asking them TO try something, can be a winning strategy.

"I know you don't normally like ***insert food item here***, but this is REALLY tasty! Would you try a bite? For me? If you don't like it, there is no harm no foul!"

That has worked for me in the past. It IS manipulation… but sometimes manipulation is necessary for us… we might not like it… but what are you going to do?

For the record… that tactic has introduced me to many dishes that I now adore!

Another good way is to go to a buffet… there is bound to be SOMETHING your Aspie can eat, and you have an opportunity to find others.

P.S. I advise that you find an Indian food buffet… The food has pleasant textures; colors; it is flavorful and still mild.

11 – Autistic Spectrum Individuals and Sexuality

It doesn't matter who you talk to, EVERYONE wants to fit in, to be loved, to be wanted. It is a basic HUMAN need. In spite of the fact that people OFTEN (this is not a blanket statement… it does not mean all non-AS individuals) treat Autistic Spectrum individuals differently than they do others, we ARE human. As a result, we have the same desires and drives as other humans. As a result of the dehumanizing treatment, disrespect and (sometimes) abuse that is thrown our way, it is harder for your Aspie to feel that they are worthy of the love and attention that we all crave so deeply.

Autism Spectrum disorders make certain aspects of personal interactions difficult at best. As I have discussed previously, the world of NT to AS communication is a veritable mine field. The anxiety and distress of failing at social interactions can truly scar the psyche of your Aspie.

Let's talk about Post Traumatic Stress Disorder. PTSD Symptoms can manifest within a short time, or take years… PTSD symptoms are normally grouped into one of three categories – intrusive memories, avoidance and numbing, and increased anxiety or a heightened emotional state. (These are according to the Mayo clinic).

Symptoms of Intrusive Memories
- flashbacks
- reliving the traumatic event
- troubling dreams focused on the event
- Does this sound like Aspie behavior? I thought so.

Symptoms of Avoidance and Emotional Numbing
- Avoidance of talking about the traumatic event
- Emotional detachment

- Avoiding activities once enjoyed
- Memory issues
- Trouble concentrating
- Difficulty maintaining relationships

Again, I ask… does this sound like Aspie behavior?

Symptoms of Anxiety and Heightened Emotional States
- Anger
- Irritability
- Overwhelming guilt or shame
- Self-destructive behaviors
- Trouble sleeping
- Being easily startled or frightened
- Hearing or seeing things that aren't there

One last time… Your Aspie has some of the same behaviors… doesn't he?

I have a theory. It is a personal theory, but I believe it is accurate. It is based on years of personal introspection and observation coupled with conversations with other Aspies. The theory is that Aspies (most if not all) have PTSD in reference to interpersonal relationships to one extent or another.

It can be a perilous journey – both for the Aspie and those who choose to love them.

Regardless of whether or not my theory is correct, interpersonal relationships are hard for Aspies.

Sexuality is a difficult concept on the best of days, even without Asperger's Syndrome. I could cover all of the aspects – Straight, Bisexual, Homosexual, Gender-queer, Gender-fluid, sapiosexual and more… But most of that is irrelevant when looking at the big picture.

Support your Aspie in their gender identity… You might not understand how they feel or how they identify themselves, gender-wise… Your job, if you truly care, is to love and accept them – unconditionally. That being said, chances are that your Aspie will fall into one of three categories of sexual desire – Asexual, Normal, and Hypersexual.

Asexual
Asexuality is non-sexuality. It literally the lack of sexual impulse, attraction or feeling. Some have posited that asexuality is actually a form of sexuality along with the (AND THIS LIST IS THE CLINICALLY ACCEPTED LIST – SO NO HATE MAIL) traditional forms of sexuality – heterosexuality, homosexuality, and bisexuality.

A study conducted in 2004 placed the prevalence of asexuality at 1%. I believe that number is a great deal higher among Aspies. (This opinion comes from a series of conversations on several of the sites I am on.)

Asexuals demonstrate behaviors that may sound odd… They abstain from sexual activity AND from celibacy… Both of which are inherently sexual behaviors. Celibacy requires a sexual identity and desire to engage sexual behavior – so that it CAN be denied. Some asexual people do engage in sexual activity despite lacking a desire for sex or sexual attraction, due to a variety of reasons, such as a desire to please romantic partners or a desire to have children.

"Normal"
Normal is that… normal. The dictionary defines normal as "conforming to the standard or the common type; usual; not abnormal; regular; natural."

Your Aspie may have all the standard hormonal and sexual desires of a person of their orientation.

Hypersexual

Hypersexuality is marked by extreme or frequent sexual urges. The desire for sexual activity can be described as intense as many of the urges associated with Obsessive Compulsive Disorder. There are a few medical conditions that have Hypersexuality listed as one the symptoms, but in most cases, there is no known cause.

Mental health problems such as bipolar disorder can give rise to Hypersexuality, as can certain drugs (Rx) that affect social and sexual inhibitions in some people. Couple Hypersexuality with the improper social behaviors associated with Asperger's Syndrome, and there can be some severe problems for your Aspie.

No matter which of the three (Asexual, Normal, or Hypersexual) your Aspie falls into, you can be in for a bumpy ride. If your Aspie is a friend, you can anticipate irritation, depression and anxiety when they are dealing with the following issue.

Aspies in relationships will be dealing with these issues on a daily basis. If you are in a relationship with your Aspie, you need to be acutely aware of their sexual proclivities… An Asexual may engage to please you… but will find little, if any enjoyment. A Normal will enjoy it all with you…

A Hypersexual can be a chore for anyone other than another Hypersexual. The average Hypersexual, unless there are mitigating circumstances, will have a libido off the charts. Sexual thoughts will be intrusive to the point of disrupting normal function… at all hours of the day… Without stopping… If you are not ready to be engaged in sexual activities this much… you may want to choose someone else or discuss other arrangements…

Many Hypersexuals have to have a second play partner to ameliorate the stresses of being with them.

No matter where on this spectrum your Aspie is on, you need to be completely open and honest with them. You also need to be able to view it all the same way that an Aspie does… If your needs are not getting met, but you wish to maintain the relationship – unusual steps may need to be taken… A playmate for you if your Asexual is unable to meet your needs… a playmate for your Aspie if your hypersexual is wearing you out.

If steps like these seem to be excessive… Then you may want to step away. I know it's harsh, but it might be necessary. When you are in a relationship with an Aspie, sometimes one must take an extreme stance… Your needs or your Aspies needs may have to take precedence over a balanced and mutual handling of these issues…

12 – Your Aspie and Special Interests

Aspies (in fact, all high functioning autistics) have obsessive behaviors and interests. In the Aspie community, the term "Special Interests" has been adopted to refer to these behaviors. Special interests are exactly what they sound like – an interest that holds the attention of our scattered thought patterns. The reason these are "Special" interests is that holding our attention is not an easy task. (ADHD, or similar symptomology, runs rampant among Aspies.

Hans Asperger described the Aspies in his study as "Little Professors." This is because Aspies have the aforementioned Special Interests. Our brains latch on to a specific topic and applies the powers of hyper-focus and Obsessive Compulsive behaviors to it and research, absorb, dissect, analyze, interpolate, and internalize every aspect of the Special Interest in question.

What this means is that your Aspie will talk about it. A lot. Actually… A lot doesn't even begin to cover it. Your Aspie will babble about it. Incessantly. Without ceasing. Ad nauseum. Ad infinitum. To the point that you will want to strangle them. And then they will babble about it until your eyes glaze. Then, they will babble about it til your ears bleed. And then… Guess what? They will babble some more.

It will be frustrating, in the extreme, for you.

If you have an Autistic Spectrum individual in your life, you need to accept this particular behavior. Moreover, you need to revel in it.

Before I cover the mechanisms behind Special Interests… Let's put things into perspective.

Neurotypicals like to talk about sports, relationships, shopping trips, religion and politics. I am sure that you enjoy talking about these topics. Now, think back to the last time that someone talked to you about one of these things… one of them that you have no interest in. The conversation was almost intolerable, wasn't it? Now… Think about how often you have yammered on about these same things to your Aspie.

So… if you can be polite to your NT friends about their interests, and you are in an interpersonal relationship with an Aspie, then you need to be as supportive of them as your NT friends. The problem with our special interests is that we engage in them the same way we do everything else… 150% or not at all.

Special Interests are bewildering to everyone – even us. We tend to be classified as emotionless… or at least, more logical, than the average person. A lot of people say that this reduces the intensity of our emotions. They would be wrong. We feel as deeply and as intensely as any Neurotypical. We simply have a more difficult time processing those emotions and an even more difficult time expressing those same emotions. This difficulty in externalizing our feelings can make things difficult for us. Since most of our emotions end up internalized, we can end up with them reaching a boiling point.

Now, think about this… when we discover a Special Interest, we are externalizing an emotional response.

I know, intense, right?

Now, let's talk about some of the mechanisms involved.

Endorphins are chemicals released by the brain. They are neurotransmitters, natural pain pain killers and relieve stress… Or rather, they act to counter the chemical causes of stress and ameliorate the symptoms of stress issues on the brain.

Intense biological studies of the brain have revealed that the same endorphins are released when fulfilling an obsession or engaging in the obsessive behaviors associated with OCD as are released by the brain when Neurotypicals fall in love.

Think about the emotions and sensations associated with falling in love. The excitement making your heart pound. You get butterflies in your stomach. You get a pleasant tingle. It feels good. It feels REALLY good.

I want you to think about that. I only have myself as an example to work with here… but I want you to think about this… I get the same feeling when I talk about quantum physics, film making, RC cars, gaming, my collections and writing as you do when you are in love.

Simply put, the presence, exercise, and tackling of a special interest for an Aspie, makes us feel better. It allows us a way to vent emotional pressure, stress relief and more. We are finally able to talk about an emotionally charged topic without difficulty.

Further – studies have linked chronic pain to Autistic Spectrum disorders. No one is quite sure why this is… I have theories, but they are only observational, without corroborating evidence as to a cause. Needless to say, almost every Aspie I have ever spoken to (myself included) has problems with chronic pain. Endorphins are natural pain killers. As a result, engaging in our special interests can and does actually improve physical functioning.

Special interests are different from standard Obsessive Behaviors. Compulsive behaviors are intrusive and are RARELY enjoyable… (there are some exceptions, but not many). Compulsive Behaviors associated with OCD are compulsions that prevent normal function and can outright interfere with enjoyment of everyday things. Special Interests share many of the same compulsive components as OCD… but they are FUN. A thing that OCD cannot claim.

So… you have a basic inkling of what it is like to have special interests. Please do not view this as dismissive, but it is an inkling only… it is not possible for someone who does not have OCD to understand what a compulsive behavior truly is. The closest metaphor I can come up with is that it is akin to breathing. Try holding your breath until you pass out. You can't, because your nerves carry a compulsion to breathe.

Now that you have an idea of what it is like… There are some other things that you will eventually notice with your Aspie. A few Special Interests will be permanent. (this is VERY few). Most of the time, you will be inundated with one topic and then suddenly, your Aspie will start in on a new Interest – one you've never head them talk about.

As with all stimulus, the brain adjusts to all stimuli. So, eventually, interests will fade. It takes more and more of the special interest just to maintain the connection to our endorphins. Eventually… the brain stops responding to that stimulus and that Special Interest is tapped out. eventually the endorphin response fades and we're left standing there… empty… So we have to develop a new one. This is an instinctive action, and we don't even know we're doing it. It's a compulsion that we can't fight and most of us wouldn't dream of trying.

Then we discover our new Special interest and we pursue it with passion. We research, experience and devour it. We push it into our brains, our souls and into our very veins… EXACTLY like a drug.

We are addicts, plain and simple. But so are NTs. NTs are addicted to emotions and their own endorphins and have a lot more and easier ways to achieve that endorphin production.

Take those Special Interests and add in the OCD triggered by the process and you will see that Aspies have NO CHOICE but to engage in this behavior – as annoying as it can be for the NTs in our lives.

I said that this produces many of the same feelings and sensations as being in love. Having been one of the lucky Aspies to have experienced complete, unconditional love (of the romantic kind), I can confirm that this is true. I want you to imagine this… Imagine a life without feeling that thrill of being in love.

Now… imagine that you have the ability to claim that power once again… something that TRULY brings you joy. That is what our special interests are to us.

As an NT in a relationship with an Aspie, you have a hard row to hoe. You have to accept that this is how we are. We don't WANT to be this way, but it is how we are. So, you have to accept it… No… if you want your Aspie to thrive, you have to revel in it. You can't cringe when we bring up our interests… we don't want to do it… we need to…

Also, keep in mind… if we are sharing our Special Interest with you… you have been let in. You are trusted and cared about. We don't even bother to talk to those people who we don't a) have an emotional attachment to or b) see as someone worth your time. By nattering on and on and on… and on and on… and on about their Special Interest, your Aspie is saying, in their own odd way, I care about and respect you.

If you have an Autistic Spectrum individual in your life, and they bring IT up… if you feel it is intolerable… think about the emotions and sensations associated with endorphins and ask yourself… "would my Aspie deny me the ability to feel what it is like to be in love?"

So… you have an Aspie in your life. At least, that is a safe-ish assumption since you are reading this. It is also, I believe, a safe assumption that you are looking for a certain amount of understanding. To facilitate this, I am going to dispel some myths about Asperger's Syndrome as well as laying down some history.

Hans Asperver was an Austrian pediatrician. In 1944, he described the behavior of four subjects (all boys) that shared similar symptoms. These symptoms would later be classified as Asperger's Syndrome. It went unknown until 1981 when Lorna Wing (an English doctor) published case studies of a group of children that displayed the same set of symptomes.

As you know… Or may not know… when multiple (two is considered multiple) studies produce similar or identical results and symptoms, it is a big deal. It is establishing a pattern. Patterns are how we, as humans, work… further, they allow us to classify mental and physical issues… Symptoms are a pattern.

In spite of the furor this caused (furor being a relative term) in the psychological community… it took eleven years for it to be added to the International Classification of Diseases (ICD-10) and thirteen years to be added to the Diagnostic and Statistical Manual of Mental Disorders (DSM-IV)

Asperger's is classified as a pervasive developmental disorder. According to www.thefreedictionary.com pervasive developmental disorders are "Any of several disorders, such as autism and Asperger's syndrome, characterized by severe deficits in many areas of development, including social interaction and communication, or by the presence of repetitive, stereotyped behaviors. Such disorders are usually evident in the first years of life and are often associated with some degree of mental retardation."

Aspies, by definition, don't have deficits of language or cognition. If either of these are present, the individual will be diagnosed with Autism. We do, however have issues with interacting, communicating and connecting with others. We are also unable to pick up on social cues.

Some say we are unable to express our emotions. I disagree with this. Due to our inability pick up on social cues, Aspies have never learned how to express our emotions in a way that is easily understood by Neurotypicals. On a personal note: I have actually been told that there is "No way" that I can feel the way I do or that I am capable of the things I know about myself.

Aspies will often exist at the extremes of behavior: Either they are orderly, obsessive and metered and can have tantrums or meltdowns if things are not "Just So" – or – their life is a whirlwind of chaos and disorder and will have a lot of problems dealing with the day to day tings. This is a general statement, not an absolute – like all things Autistic, it is a spectrum.

Social ineptitude can lead to awkwardness, complications, rivalry and even trouble.

There has been a lot of media attention to Asperger's in recent years… And and as with anything that's in the news, misconceptions have come into being.

Myth #1 – an Asperger's child will grow out of it.
For some reason, people have started to believe that Asperger's is childhood disease. As such, there is an unfounded belief that children will grow out of it. This is blatantly untrue… to a certain extent. If your Aspie is lucky, they will encounter someone in their life who is able to translate NT to

Aspie. If they can find that, and that person is patient and intuitive, they can educate their Aspie. It is rare, but it does happen.

Simply put – Aspies can't do the social things that NTs do intuitively. When a Neurotypical walks into a social situation, within moments they KNOW what is going on. Because your Aspie cannot intuit these situations, they are often lost – BUT they are called social SKILLS for a reason. Skills can be learned.

So, if you have a talented and patient teacher AND an Aspie who is DETERMINED to succeed at all of this, it is possible for them to learn how to wade into the social arena with a certain amount of savvy and skill. This does not, by any means, mean that the Aspie will grow out of it… It only means that they have the capability to learn certain aspects of social interactions. However, the underlying mechanisms and symptomology of Asperger's Syndrome will still be in evidence and attendance for their entire lives.

As of yet, there is no cure for Autistic Spectrum disorders.

Myth #2 – Aspies lack Empathy
In recent years, Psychologists have divided empathy into two different classifications – Emotional Empathy and Cognitive Empathy.

Emotional Empathy is basically the dictionary definition of empathy: the intellectual identification with or vicarious experiencing of the feelings, thoughts, or attitudes of another. Your Aspie is capable of this… and in fact is extremely skilled at it.

The second form of Empathy is Cognitive Empathy. What is Cognitive Empathy? It is the ability to REALIZE what emotion a person is experiencing. Since we miss the social cues, expressions and microexpressions indicative of the emotions being experienced by another person.

Tell your Aspie that you are sad, and they will demonstrate adequate empathy... but please do not expect them to be a mind reader.

Myth #3 – Aspies do not make Eye Contact
It can seem that way, honestly. But your Aspie WILL make eye contact... However, like with ALL social interactions, it is often in inappropriate or odd ways.

They may make fleeting eye contact and then focus on another thing. In my case it is because it is intensely uncomfortable for me to make prolonged eye contact with people that I don't know... In nature, prolonged eye contact can be a prelude to mating, flirtation, a challenge of social status, or a prelude to violence. The Aspie mind freaks out... trying to decide whether to flee, have sex or fight.

Often, we become intensely aware that someone else is trying to force eye contact or REALLY wants to look us in the eyes... and we over compensate... STARING.

Myth #4 – Aspies are aloof or un-interested in other people.
As an Aspie, I can dispel this myth. I have spoken to a great number of Aspies. Guess what? We are just like you... we want and need interaction and socialization. It is hard. We don't get the social cues, laugh at inappropriate times, are perceived to be without empathy, are perceived to be talking about ourselves constantly (when in reality, we are gabbling on about our special interests)...

In reality, at times, we don't realize that others have different thoughts and feelings than we do. And since it is considered rude in NT society to correct someone, we never see the fault in this assumption and NTs assume that we are arrogant and uncaring.

We also, often, are not equipped with the proper repertoire of emotional responses which leads to more social awkwardness as NT feeds off of Aspie and vice versa in a vicious cycle.

Myth #5 – Aspies have social phobia.
While most Aspies do struggle with anxiety, on the whole, they don't have social phobia. In many cases, it may seem that way, but in all honesty, it is that parties and large social gatherings are RARELY engaging for us. In any group of people (except for those special groups that meet just for that interest), it is rare for an Aspie to find anyone that is interested in their Special Interests.

Further, as far as I can tell (and this is a blanket statement, not a statement of an absolute), Aspies rarely enjoy the activities that are routinely engaged in at parties – loud music, drinking, and just talking about nothing. While I know there are some Aspies that have addictive personalities and will engage in drunken debauchery, for the most part – with our sensory issues and cognitive dissonance issues – it is rare to find an Aspie that will enjoys being altered chemically.

In my case, being drunk was unpleasantly similar to many of the medications they tried me on in my youth.

What is often perceived as phobia is a case of your Aspie having no interest in the proffered activity.

Myth #6 – All Aspies are nerds, all nerds are Aspies
Many Aspies have Special Interests that are considered to be "Nerdy", but more often, our Special Interests are more

esoteric… for some reason, My Little Pony seems to be one. Special Interests can be anything… LITERALLY anything.

And, HONESTLY, most nerds are not on the spectrum – no matter what people think.

Myth #7 – Asperger's and Autism is caused by vaccines
This myth is based on an incorrect understanding of chemistry, physics and biology. Jenny McCarthy, the champion of "vaccines are the cause", also stated that gluten was the reason her son was autistic… she fed him a macrobiotic diet and it "CURED HIS AUTISM."

This… is bunk… I wanted to use stronger language, but I am making a concerted effort to be proper. Jenny McCarthy…is an idiot on this topic… and probably every other topic, but most certainly this one.

Myth #8 – Only males can have Asperger's
There are many females with Asperger's Syndrome. Many remain undiagnosed for a variety of reasons, but they still can have Asperger's. I can confirm this… My sister is an Aspie as well. Most of this has to do with the social restrictions put upon young females, and that many of the social traits of Asperger's are seen as more acceptable in a female.

Myth #9 – Asperger's doesn't exist and is just an excuse to not be a part of society
Just reading this statement makes me angry. Asperger's is real and most children desperately want to be a part of society. We don't want to be excluded, ignored, or worse – persecuted for it. (And this DOES happen). We want to be a part of society, but often… we just don't know how to do it.

Myth #10 – Aspies and Autistic Spectrum individuals are mentally retarded

The fact of the matter is that to be diagnosed with Aspergers, an individuals MUST have at lease normal intelligence. The diagnostic criteria state this clearly. If there is mental retardation, then the child will (most likely) be diagnosed with Autism.

Myth #11 – All Aspies want to be cured

This is honesty a rarity. Many Autistic Spectrum individuals feel that there is nothing wrong with them. Others think that AS is not a disease, simply being wired differently. Regardless of whether we want a cure, by the time we reach adulthood, a cure would be pretty useless… even if we could SUDDENLY make sense of the social and sensory inputs we are experiencing, by the time we are adults, these personality traits have become an intrinsic part of our psyche and who we are.

14 – Pets, The Death of and Grieving

This part of the series was planned for a long ways down the road. Things, however, do change. In my case, a beloved pet died. I thought to myself, what better time than the present, but first…

Every Aspie I know of has a thing with animals. When asked, the answer I most often receive is, "I get along with them better than I do people." It may not be clear from an NT standpoint, but it makes sense for Aspies. Animals have VERY clear body language. They react in predictable ways to set stimuli. Humans, NTs especially, seem unpredictable and volatile to the Aspie brain. They have micro-expressions that flicker across their faces, that leave us bewildered. Animals are pretty straight forward about their emotions and can be read relatively easily which is incredibly pleasing to the Autistic Spectrum Brain.

Watch an Aspie with their pets – be they cats, dogs, horses, snakes, lizards or birds. Seriously watch them. You will see an amazing amount of love, empathy and compassion directed at this animal… and the animal will respond in kind.

So, you can understand why the death of a beloved pet can be devastating to anyone. Some would argue that it would be harder for an Autistic Spectrum individual due to the fact that their routine and life are disrupted.

I have given a great many animals a happy home in my time – rats, ferrets, dogs, cats, snakes, turtles, lizards, and one Egyptian crypt spider. I loved every one of them. (Yes, even the spider). When they tied… it ripped me up inside. Your Aspie will be the same.

However, after the death of a beloved pet, your Aspie may do something that will surprise you. In most of the cases of Aspie pet's deaths that I have seen… The Aspie wants another pet VERY soon after the pet's passing.

This, to many Neurotypicals, seems to be a callous and unfeeling move on the part of their Aspie. This is not the case. I will break it down for you.

Autistic Spectrum individuals are very much creatures of habit. This makes change difficult. This is in both the coming AND the going. When you first purchase your Aspie a pet, there will be a great amount of stress involved in making the adjustment to the presence of the new family member.

It will be just as difficult to adjust to their loss, as well. Where an NT will probably shy away the concept of a "replacement pet", your Aspie may react completely differently. They will mourn the loss of their animal, but their will be a hole in their life.

This hole is a great deal deeper for the Autistic Spectrum individual than it would and NT in the same situation. I am not belittling the emotional devastation felt by anyone, but it gets more intense for the Autistic Spectrum individual because we are not only in mourning, but we are also dealing with an upset in routine.

This clash of powerful emotions can lead to tantrums, depression, anxiety, sleep problems and meltdowns.

As a defense mechanism, the Aspie brain will seek to diffuse a lot of the emotional impact. One of the primary ways to do this is to fill the holes left by the missing pet. This means getting a new one – long before an NT is able to do so. If the pet was a dog, the Aspie will want another dog. If the pet is a caged animal, it will probably be a new caged animal.

This rapid replacement of a pet doesn't mean that your Aspie didn't love them… it means that they have to fight off the cognitive dissonance that will cause further pain and suffering. Please realize that their pain is as intense as yours, if not more.

15 – Jobs, Stress and Your Aspie

It is estimated that upwards of 80% of adults with Asperger's Syndrome don't have full-time jobs. There are a great many factors that contribute to this. Some argue that it is not because we cannot do the work, but instead because of socially inappropriate behavior in the job place. While this might be true in some cases, I am not sure that this is the case in most instances.

But, for the sake of argument, let's look at the social issues facing your Aspie in the work place.

The stress of constant interpersonal interactions can cause anxiety, cognitive dissonance, and tantrums. Further, Aspies have a tendency to be focused on hard facts and truth, which means that we can be truly infuriating without meaning to be. Most Aspies, when they are certain that something is a specific way will argue it to the point of being obnoxious. (We are all guilty of it.) And the issue with this is… We don't know we're doing it. Studies of the work place show that people would rather work with pleasant and reasonable individuals, rather than someone who is always right.

When aware of it, your Aspie will try to be more accommodating and pleasant, but the inability to read social cues properly make this difficult in the extreme… we will try to plan out interactions in an attempt to fix it… but fail spectacularly… Neurotypicals don't follow the scripts in our heads.

Autistic Spectrum individuals have shown impairment of short term memory. In most cases, long term memory is outstanding – often better than Neurotypicals. This is fine in day to day life, but really will impact almost any job that I am engaged in.

Another issue that needs to be addressed is ritual and habits. These are important aspects of the Aspie and Autistic Spectrum psyche. Without clearly defined ritual and routine, it is easy for your Aspie to become overwhelmed, which leads to stress issues. Most jobs make it hard to fall into a routine, which makes it difficult for your Aspie to adjust.

Your average Aspie will have an over developed sense of duty (it took a LOT for them to get into the job market in the first place) and a stubborn streak a mile wide. This means that they will ignore the anxiety and stress… and let it build… Often to the point of being non-verbal, stimming or full on blow outs…

Further… once they realize that a job is not one they can do, they will feel horrible. This is another big reminder of how different we are… NTs do the job thing all the time, we should be able to as well. As previously discussed in this series, any reminder that we are dysfunctional can be EXTREMELY upsetting.

Yeah… This upsetting

The ideal job for an Aspie would be one that had a high degree of repetition, but also variance. I know that sounds impossible to find, but there are a few out there… Many factories allow for this… repetition on one machine and then being moved to another machine… HOWEVER, the noise and bright lights of most factory floors can be as problematic, especially if your Aspie suffers sensory issues.

Several fields that I have seen a high degree of Aspie compatibility with are drafting, computer programming, industrial arts, technical writing, language arts and the like. This is especially true if these are Special Interests for your Aspie. If they are not… DO NOT try to force these subjects on your Aspie. As I have stated previously in the Food Issues part of this series, this will only prompt Oppositional Behavior.

Typically, we don't work well in a standard work/office environment. We normally have to compensate for our deficit in social skills by becoming specialists. Since that is what we are good at (with our special interests and all), it is more than possible to make ourselves indispensable. I have found that it was better for me to make my own company and then make a reputation in my field and get paid to do what we do.

With the unemployment rate so high, it is even harder to find a job for Autistic Spectrum individuals than in previous years.

To assist, I have compiled the following list:
- Accounting
- Animal trainer or veterinary technician
- Automobile mechanic
- Bank Teller
- Building maintenance
- Building trades
- Clerk and filing jobs
- Commercial art
- Computer animation
- Computer programming
- Computer-troubleshooter and repair
- Copy Editor
- Crafts
- Data entry
- Drafting
- Engineering
- Factory Assembly work
- Inventory control

- Janitorial
- Journalism
- Lab Tech
- Lawn Care
- Librarian
- Maintenance
- Mechanical Design
- Mathematics
- Photography
- Physicist
- Recycling – sorter
- Store Shelf Stocker
- Small appliance repair
- Small engine repair
- Statistics
- Taxi Driver
- Telemarketer
- Video Game Designer
- Loading trucks in a warehouse
- Web page Design

16 – Intelligence, Neurotypicals and Relations

Intelligence is a difficult thing to measure and quantify. Modern psychology does its best, but sometimes falls short in measuring it effectively. The best measurement that is available today is the Intelligence Quotient, or IQ. This score is calculated from a set of standardized tests to asses intelligence. William Stern is responsible for the label – "IQ".

Tests are updated routinely, and the median raw score of the sample is set as 100. Due to the math involved, the score of 100 is considered average intelligence. Standard deviation is defined as 15 points up or down. Thus, by definition approximately 95 percent of the population will score between 70-130 which is within two standard deviations of the median.

Some factors that influence IQ scores are socio-economic status, co-morbid conditions, and (to a great degree) parental IQ. While heredity seems to play a role, little is known or understood about the mechanisms of intelligence through genetics. It has been observed that parents with exceptionally high IQ can produce a child with a substandard IQ and vice versa.

Before I continue… IQ is an inaccurate and inefficient way to measure intelligence. It measures knowledge. It is very possible fore an illiterate man to have a dazzling intellect and for a MENSA member to be dumber than a bag of unassembled hammers. It is possible for a coal miner, who has never known anything beyond his environs to be smarter than all of us combined, but score poorly on the IQ test because he has never had a chance learn the facts and figures and mathematics that appear on the IQ test. For all we know, the smartest man in the world is living in the jungles of Pau Pau, New Guinea.

It is worth noting the Flynn Effect. The Flynn Effect states that every decade or so the IQ of a given area rises by an average of 3 points. This, however, is only true for the low end and has no noticeable effect on the high end of the scale.

Now that we have established the function and a the baselines, it is worth noting that the average IQ in the United States is 98.

Averages are calculated by adding together all numbers and then dividing by the number of entries in the range. That means to achieve an average score of 100, there are a lot of scores that are higher and a lot more that are lower.

From the stand point of averages, Aspies tend to be a bit more intelligent than Neurotypicals. The reason for this is this – to be diagnosed with Asperger's Syndrome, an individual cannot be mentally retarded. That means that the bell curve for Aspies does not include those of 70 IQ or less. The lowest end of the spectrum is removed from the calculations, skewing the results.

In reality, however, Aspies demonstrate the same wide array of IQ scores as Neurotypicals. Often, Aspies will appear to be more intelligent than those around them. This, however, is an illusion. Unintentionally, Aspies will guide the conversation to an area of their expertise. In this, they are no different than NTs. The conversation will invariably end up on one of the Aspie's Special Interests… This means that your Aspie will be discussing something that they are an expert in.

If you guide the conversation away from the Special Interest, your Aspie will be out of their depth. Typically this will either, a) end in your Aspie becoming exceedingly quiet, b) your Aspie listening intently, absorbing all that they can, or c) end up with your Aspie wandering off.

As near as I can tell, there are two perceptions of Aspies…

those that are open and observant enough to see the intelligence within us (which, as previously stated, is the same spectrum as NTs) and those that perceive us as less intelligent.

This evolution kind of sums up what I am saying

The latter cannot be blamed for their perceptions. Millions of years of evolution have trained them, on a genetic level to assume that someone is inferior if they are different. It is evolution in action and, until they evolve to be different, only the most intelligent are able to overcome these instincts.

What I am saying is that Aspies and NTs share a great number of traits… and intelligence is one of them. Honestly, without a common frame of reference, both NT and Aspie will consider the other to be less intelligent.

This will cause problems in NT/Aspie relations. Often One will make disparaging comments about the Other without realizing that they are more than capable enough of deciphering these thinly (if at all) veiled insults. Honestly, and it shames me to say it, this is worse coming from the Aspie to the NT.

The NT world is fraught with masks, insults, tiny lies, hidden feelings and politeness. The politeness is often an affront to one's true feelings and Aspies will have nothing to do with it. Whether this is due to an inability to process these social constructs or the Aspie's inherent need for absolutes is unclear – even to me, and I am Aspie. So, in these situations, it is far more likely that the Aspie will take action (harsh words) on these perceived and subtle slights.

To further NT/Aspie relations, we need to work to find that common ground. The NTs will need to work at being blunt, and avoid evasion and subtle jibes. The Aspie will need to keep in mind that the NT has little choice in their social nature… No more than we do in our anti-social nature. If we all work together, these issues can be avoided.

This is where awareness comes in. What this means, in a practical sense, is that the Aspie will need to advise those around them about their condition. Your Aspie needs to be careful, however… This can lead to the NTs around them perceiving this as making excuses for their behavior. Also… it can lead to your Aspie actually doing exactly that.

With understanding, however, we can make strides forward in NT/Aspie relations.

With the high rate of co-morbid conditions that accompany Asperger's syndrome, and their secondary effects, skin problems, digestion issues, joint problems and any of the complications associated with anxiety disorders, it can be a chore to make sure your Aspie is taken care of, medically speaking.

Which brings us to another issue – getting your Aspie in to treatment of any kind.

As you have probably learned by now, your Aspie is resistant to seeing the doctor. Let's take a look at some of the main reasons for this.

Aspies are creatures of truth and typically, doctors are reluctant to give more information than is needed. If, on a visit, the doctor tells your Aspie, "I suspect this is the case." Your Aspie will research the condition, symptoms, treatment options, possible medications, best places for such treatment, exceptions to the symptoms, conditions with similar symptoms and any alternative treatment alternatives.

This can be off putting to the medical professional, especially if they are not familiar with the Aspie mind. They will be, sometimes unconsciously, offended by a patient telling them all about that which they have dedicated their lives to. As a result, the health care professional will often, most of the time very subtly, change their behaviors because they are trying not to slap the offending Aspie. (This is a state of being we often inspire in others) Your Aspie will pick up on this… we are, after all, pattern seeking machines. The change in doctor behavior will strike a wrong note in the already discordant experience of a doctor's visit.

Further, your Aspie, due to his research, may present treatment options, exceptions or alternative diagnoses that your doctor did not consider or was unaware of. Medicine is an eternally evolving field, and without CONSTANT study, it is difficult for a medical professional to keep up with all the changes. Often, when your Aspie makes a suggestion, the doctor will leave the room. I can assure you that they have hopped on an internet capable computer and verified what has been said. The NT reaction to this situation is often to become upset. For reasons Aspies cannot comprehend, the NT will take this as an attempt to show them up or prove that we know more than they do.

These situations lead to the NT being upset. The responses to the changes in NT vocal patterns and nonverbal cues will often upset the Aspie and lead them to believe that the NT doctor is being hostile, which will make your Aspie agitated and difficult to deal with in those situations. Some anxiety disorders can actually convert this unease into paranoia which will lead to your Aspie refusing to accept diagnoses, prescriptions and treatment plans from this specific care provider.

There are other complications to doctor's visits… let's look at it from the Aspie standpoint.

Here are the issues as we see them:
- Doctors rarely seem to REALLY know what they are doing. The medical health professional will assure you that they know what they are doing… The issue is that medicine, in spite of its being referred to as the Medical Sciences, is more of an art. With the countless body chemistries in the world, it is hard to say that one medication or treatment plan is ABSOLUTELY the way to go. Expressing that to your average NT will result in panic and doubt, so doctors make it a point to avoid the topic. Since they come from a point of authority,

switching up treatment plans for an NT patient is a great deal easier than it is for an Autistic Spectrum individual. As such, your Aspie will get the impression that the doctor is clueless.

- Doctors operate on a double standard. You will be scheduled for a specific time. If you are more than 10 minutes late, you will lose your appointment. Yet, when you get there, you are often required to wait for hours. Your Aspie, with a few notable exceptions, has an over-developed sense of fairness and this will be upsetting to your Aspie.

- Doctors lie. Partially, this has to do with the aforementioned process of locating the proper medications or treatment plan. Mostly it has to do with the little lies that are told in an effort to facilitate treatment. Statements like, "This won't hurt a bit," "You're going to feel a slight pinch," "I'll be back in just a minute," and "You will feel a slight pressure," are upsetting when they precede pain, exceptional discomfort or a 25 minute wait. Your Aspie will feel betrayed by this behavior.

- Doctors assume that they know best. They DO know what to do… But their approach of "do what I say" doesn't work with most Aspies.

- Most doctors don't listen. Aspies tend to be very aware of issues dealing with their own bodies. They may not be terribly emotionally aware, but their bodies are what they carry around with them all the time. Doctors will dismiss certain symptoms and pains as psychosomatic when they are real issues. When dealing with mental and emotional issues, mental health professionals will doubt certain aspects of what the Aspie tells them. They believe that either a) the Aspie is looking for attention or specific meds which the Mental Heath Care provider are sure they don't need b) that the Aspie cannot possibly think or believe what they do or c) that the Aspie is not capable of the thoughts, actions or feelings they are experiencing. When the Aspie is told this, they take it personally. We spend our entire lives with people not believing us, assuming that we are exaggerating or worse, lying. I can tell you, Aspies take very badly to being considered liars.

Most doctors don't know important things about Aspies.
- We are sensitive to medications – anything with a behavioral element will often be overblown due to the disorder.
- When we have side effects… we have them to the fullest extent possible.
- Any medication that changes the equilibrium of he body (i.e. all of them) will cause anxiety and uncertainty. When the equilibrium of your Aspie's body is thrown off, they will NOT like the effect (at least at first) even if it is beneficial.
- We seek to understand. While an NT will accept a procedure, medication or treatment plan without question, if it is not explained to the Aspie… and I mean really explained… the treatment, the reasons and the mechanisms… The Aspie will assume that there is something that is being hidden from them – which will lead to your Aspie becoming stubborn and even oppositional.

So, the best plan of action is to search for a doctor. It takes time and patience… but you have to find the RIGHT doctor. While setting up the initial appointment, it is best to mention that you are setting up an appointment for a special needs adult, someone that needs special attention.

Often, it may be best to search out a doctor that specializes in Autism Spectrum individuals. There are very few of them, but they ARE out there… a general practitioner that deals regularly with Autistic Spectrum individuals will have a grasp of what it is to deal with the trials and tribulations of treating your Aspie. It may be a trial in and of itself to FIND the right doctor for this… but it will make medical treatment FAR easier for you in the future.

18 – Rules to Help Aspies Navigate the NT World

This is a departure from the rest of the series. I have been writing this primarily to assist Neurotypicals in understanding their Aspies. In this part, I will be imparting some of the myriad social rules that we are inundated with throughout our lives. These will seem nonsensical to most NTs, but I assure you these make sense to Aspies.

These are in no specific order, but they are all (and I mean ALL) appropriate and have bearing on my life. I have shared them with some Aspies in the past, and every one has agreed that these are important.

There is no small amount of humor in this list… But that is part of why these are so important.

1. We do not talk about fight club.

2. No… Seriously… We DO NOT talk about Fight Club. This is both humor and a rule of my friends. We do not talk about Fight Club, Memento, the philosophy of the Matrix movies or the movie Oscar.

3. There is no rule number 3.

4. Don't touch strangers. The police frown on this.

5. If someone asks you for their positive qualities, "Useful" is not an acceptable answer. I am REALLY not sure why, but I assure you… It is unacceptable.

6. Blink. Hyperfocus makes the NTs around you nervous. It has been explained to me that normal people blink in accordance to their thought patterns, not when their eyes need it.

7. Dancing in public is only acceptable when everyone else is doing it... and when there is music.

8. Finish the sentences you start… corollary: Start sentences you finish.

9. When people ask "What did you do this weekend?", they really don't want to know. This, according to my pet NTs… is called being polite. The only proper answer is "Fine."

10. Ask before you pet someone else's dog. You may be gifted with the ability to relate to animals exceptionally well, but they don't know that. Corollary: do not discipline someone else's pet.

11. Inside voice means don't yell… I used to think that it was my inside voice because I was inside… so… no yelling… No matter how excited you are. Corollary: it is not acceptable to yell just because we are outside. Corollary to the Corollary: this is not a request to spout your inner monologue.

12. If you dislike someone, and someone else asks, answering "I hate them," evidently, is unacceptable. I really don't know why… This seems to be an NT trait – to ask a question that they don't want the answer to. They will ask this in hopes you will confirm what they think or feel about the person. Personally, I say, "I would not spend time with them."

13. If someone tells you "It is art.", and then asks for an opinion, the only appropriate response is to nod appreciatively. As with number 12… it is evidently (I have been assured) considered rude and insulting to give the NTs an honest critique of the work.

14. Don't pace around NTs… even though you are just thinking…it makes them nervous. As near as I can tell, they view pacing as a form of aggression.

15. Grammar Nazis are not welcome, except on a forum on grammar. Corollary: Learn to spell; learn to use your spell check; learn to use proper grammar… Beat them at their own game. Corollary to the Corollary: Don't Grammar Nazi others (THAT IS A VERB IF I SAY IT IS)… and when Grammar Nazi'd… ignore it…

16. Don't talk about friends unless everyone in the conversation knows them. This just confuses the NTs around you. I know with the egocentricity we are capable of, it can seem that EVERYONE knows everyone we know… but I promise you… it is just not true.

17. Wear a coat in winter, even if you aren't cold. I don't get this one either… but it makes NTs uncomfortable…

18. Stabbing someone with a plastic spork because they stole a french fry is inappropriate. Corollary: Stealing french fries because someone does not have or would not stab you with a fork is also inappropriate.

19. Offer suggestions… This means, "I would try **this** in this situation," NOT "You should." You should is considered arrogant.

20. Just because you want to be in a conversation doesn't mean people want you in it. Talk to your pet NTs and ask them to explain how you can tell when this is the case… and APPLY that knowledge… It will make your social life a great deal easier.

21. Truth is not the most important thing in most conversations. Hyperbole, simile and metaphor are normal human activities. These may be mystifying to us at times, but the NTs around you will engage in them constantly… Try to enjoy it.

22. "Do you like my outfit?" or "Does this make me look fat?" are both traps… DON'T ANSWER!

23. Do not ask questions that you don't want to answer… Seriously… Don't

24. Being honest is not the same as being an asshole. Try to be sensitive. One can be incredibly honest and still be sensitive to the personality, gender, religion, and feelings of another.

25. No matter what they say, NTs can't multitask well. Nor can they think objectively. They will all say they can. Smile and nod, and let them believe it. Corollary: Chances are… neither can you… there are very few people, NT or otherwise that can truly multitask with any degree of success.

26. You can't conform… Honestly… you are wired differently. So… be different. Be a LOT different. Being very different means you are an individual… being a little different makes them notice the little things a lot more

27. The teacher may be wrong. Do not correct them in front of the class. Regardless of the truth of the situation, you are undermining their ability to teach. The NT students in the class will question every right thing that they say. This is NOT cool.

28. "Don't get me started on **blank**" means you are supposed to prompt them on that topic. Don't ask me why… I don't get it… I have been assured that this is a truism.

29. The rules of NTs will sometimes make no sense at all. These are considered a non-optional social contract. You have to do them anyway. Corollary: whether you believe you are "just wired differently" or feel that Autistic Spectrum disorders are a disease, you cannot expect every NT to conform to your social conventions when they can't even agree on pizza toppings.

30. Don't be ashamed to tell people, "Hey… I have Asperger's Syndrome. Can you explain what I am missing here?". You would be surprised at how often they will accommodate and explain.

31. If you have asked a question twice… they don't want to talk about it. Let it go. No… seriously… Drop it.

32. Try not to interrupt… I know it's hard… but it pisses everyone else off.

33. If someone insults you (and they will) just smile… they don't even know they did it!

34. Talk. Not constantly, but if you are silent, most NTs think you consider yourself better than they are… while this may be true, they don't need to think it. Corollary: Don't talk to much… If you do, most NTs will think you consider yourself better than they are.

35. Tolerate slang. Don't get uppity about it, and for god's sake, don't try it.

36. Don't ask people how old they are. Evidently, this is rude.

37. Try to smile. I know it doesn't feel natural… but if they don't see it, NT people think you're angry all the time. Honestly… practice in the mirror… with friends… Your smile will be odd if not practiced and refined.

38. If someone asks what you think about their work… they want an ego stroking, not an honest response. Corollary: They can't handle the truth!

39. Even if the answer to a question is one word, say more… they think verbally expedient answers (one word) are rude.

40. Rhetorical questions are not meant to be answered… Why do they ask them? I don't know. How do you know they are rhetorical questions? Ask yourself… do they know the answer or is it RIGHT THERE IN FRONT OF THEM? If the answer is yes, it was rhetorical… Corollary: If they ask what you think is a rhetorical question more than twice… chances are, it wasn't rhetorical.

41. Try not to be pedantic. Do not pontificate. Try not to use a big word when a diminutive word will suffice.

42. Arguments are very rarely about what is being discussed. There is something else there. The average NT doesn't want to exchange ideas and evolve their standpoint. They want to fight. I am told this is cathartic. If even if you are right… you will lose.

43. Don't try to emulate NT fashion… this is a recipe for

failure. If you do, expect to be a meme of some sort.

44. It is not okay to do cartwheels in a kilt. Ever.

45. NTs like to use the term friend for anyone they have met. Don't tell them that they are "an acquaintance at best". This offends them.

46. Don't talk to yourself in public. I know it's hard, but don't do it. Corollary: If you cannot help doing this, don't look at people when you do it. They will think you are talking to them.

47. Do not get into religious discussions with ANYONE. Their responses will not be rational, and you cannot win.

48. Taking your own utensils to a restaurant is frowned upon.

49. Don't sniff your food before eating it. The cook gets offended. IF you have to sniff… do so with an appreciative smile and a deep inhalation. They will interpret it as enjoyment and be pleased.

50. Conversations evolve as they happen. That means the topics will change. Don't insist on bringing it back to the original topic.

51. Reciprocate. When they ask "How are you?" They want their turn, too.

52. Don't do anything unless you are comfortable. It will show. Corollary: Do something that scares you once a day.

53. Nod while you listen. Otherwise, they think you don't

understand and will beat that dead horse into a bloody jelly-like substance. Corollary: Comments like that last one are not acceptable at the dinner table. (Or so I have been informed)

54. Just because you love reptiles doesn't mean they do. Don't surprise them with your baby. Give them some warning.

55. When you have guests, leaving them alone is not hospitality, and they will get offended.

56. Always say the out loud part out loud. Do not assume they heard you thinking. Corollary: Leave the inside part inside. Saying it out loud can be awkward.

57. NTs, on the whole, do not know the meaning of the word irony. They do not like it when you point this out.

58. Even though they fit the classical definition of the word, unborn children are not to be referred to as parasites. Evidently, this is rude.

59. Never forget: you are not alone… even NTs feel awkward in social situations at times.

19 – To Cure or Not to Cure?

The following statements are from personal experience and reasoning. I have Asperger's Syndrome and am considered High Functioning by most standards. So, I can only speak for myself as the information applies to other High Functioning individuals. I do not have a frame of reference, nor do I claim to speak for those with greater impairments than I. I do, however, feel that my understanding of the underlying mechanisms of Autistic Spectrum behavior do carry through logically and should be considered to have at least a modicum of validity.

To cure; or not to cure? That really is THE question.

As autism awareness grows, this question becomes more electrifying by the day. Groups like Autism Speaks are out there and they have been pushing for a cure to autism. Many parents are thrilled by the possibility.

There are several issues at work here – not the least of which is that Autism Speaks, as a group, is upsetting to most Autistic Spectrum individuals. There are numerous reasons why, and Autism Speaks just doesn't seem to get it. The following reasons are my OPINION and NOT presented as fact.

- Let's start by looking at the big one… Autism Speaks has used legal threats to silence Autistic Spectrum individuals who have spoken out against the group. I don't really know why they react like this, but it seems to be counter to their stated purpose – to represent Autistic Spectrum individuals to the world. Bullying is something that Autistic Spectrum individuals deal with at different points in their lives and the irony of an Autism advocacy group that engages in that very behavior seems lost upon them. Here are two examples: Autism Speaks threatens 14 year old for parody site –

and – Autism speaks threatens illegal action against Autism Spectrum individual who makes a t-shirt speaking out against them. It just doesn't sit well with most of us.

- There is no accountability for money to Autism Speaks. They have no transparency in their book keeping. Unlike most similar charities and advocacy groups (not just for autism), Autism Speaks does not reveal what they are doing with the money. This would not be an issue if it wasn't clear that they use a lot of it to bully Autistic Spectrum individuals as above.
- It is hard for us to believe that Autism Speaks truly speaks for us. Autism Speaks produced a movie called "Autism Every Day." In this movie, one of the BOARD members of Autism Speaks states that she considered driving off a bridge with her Autistic Spectrum daughter in it and the only reason she doesn't is her other daughter. She contemplated MURDER-SUICIDE because her daughter was Autistic… Don't believe me? Here's a link to the clip – Watch it on YouTube. I hope you can see how this can be damaging to their reputation.
- Autism speaks has routinely portrayed autism in a terribly negative light. They have used words like "disaster", "epidemic", and "hopeless". This negative portrayal of Autistic Spectrum individuals has caused a great many people difficulty in social situations. I, myself, have experienced this blow-back. On their website (at least in the past, I have not looked recently.) Autism Speaks compared the rise in documented cases of Autistic Spectrum Disorders to cancer and HIV… This is offensive because these are conditions that, left untreated, will result in death. No one, to date, has died from an untreated case of Autism.
- Autism Speaks tries to portray itself as THE authority on autism. They claim to "Speak for Autism." Yet their

advertisements and information are fear based propaganda that focus on the negative impact that autism has on families, portraying us all as nightmares to be around. As many family and friends of Autistic Spectrum individuals can attest, this is not the case. There are challenges, but we are not a nightmare to be endured.

- The financial expenditures they have revealed show a great deal on possible treatments and cures, but very little on what they refer to as "Family Services." Cognitive behavioral therapy and developing coping skills and mechanisms that are necessary for proper functioning in Neurotypical society. Almost all mental health professionals agree that these are the most effective treatment plans and options… and this is what Autism Speaks refers to as "Family Services."

- Lastly, and this is the biggest sticking point for me is that Autism Speaks does not have one Autistic Spectrum individual on their board. They are claiming to speak for Autism without the voice of one of us. How can you make decisions for an entire (STATISTICALLY SIGNIFICANT) portion of the population without one of us there to advise?

Contrary to what I have written thus far, this is not an entry speaking out against Autism Speaks. Autism Speaks just happens to be the largest Autism cure advocacy on the planet. They push for prenatal testing and prevention as well as a bio-medical cure.

When reading their materials, it is unclear what they intend with the concept of autism prevention. However, considering it is almost always listed in conjunction with pre-natal testing, one can draw a logical conclusion. They may mean to introduce a retrovirus, in vitro, to rewrite the DNA of the unborn child, but considering that this technology is many years or even decades off… This is unlikely. I have read a lot of their materials… And, honestly, it feels a lot like eugenics reminiscent of 1940s Germany.

They push for a cure when we don't even know what causes Autistic Spectrum Disorders.

However… Let's say that we have a cure. We live in an age where we can rewrite DNA with a machine or a retrovirus or something else equally science fiction-like. This is possible in the future, but not today… but this is a hypothetical situation.

Having this technology means that children diagnosed with Autistic Spectrum disorders in the womb could be cured before birth. The upshot of this is that they would have none of the developmental issues that come with Autism and be able to lead perfectly normal – Neurotypical – lives. I am all for this.

Well, mostly. Procedures like this are guaranteed to be prohibitively expensive. DNA tests cost $500-$600 a piece. To create a cure like this, a full DNA work up has to be done. Then the offending genetic code has to be identified. Then a custom DNA strand has to be built. After that, the DNA strand will have to be introduced into a viral medium. This virus would then be cultured and introduced into the host body where they will inject the new DNA strand into the cells of the body.

If it sounds like something out of science fiction… that is because it is. Like many devices we use today, what was once science fiction is now science fact. (Cell phones, iPads, credit cards, travel to the moon). We are standing at a precipice of ability and discovery… which is to say, this technology is within view, if not reach.

As with many other procedures, since Autism is not a life threatening condition, it will most likely be considered a voluntary procedure and will not be covered by insurance. As such, this cure will not be available to any but the rich. I'm not going to debate the ethics of this as that is not the point of this essay, and you probably do not want to experience the invective that this topic would invoke.

So… Let's make another assumption… it is inexpensive, easy to produce and available to everyone. I am all for it. That means no children would have to go through the difficulties I did when growing up. That would be absolutely awesome an I am all for it.

But what about the adults? What about those that have learned to live with Autistic Spectrum disorders. Simply put, even if we received a cure – something that fixed the underlying mechanisms of our Autistic Spectrum Disorder, it would do us little good.

According to studies, a child's mind formed incredibly early. One study actually states that personality is codified as early as 3 years of age. (study located here) However, by the time Autistic Spectrum individuals reach a level of intellectual maturity, we have conditioned ourselves into a specific set of behaviors.

This is to say that, if someone cured my Asperger's Syndrome today… I would behave largely like I do today. I would pick up on social cues and be a bit more comfortable in social situations, but I would still be outspoken, brutally honest, intolerant of being touched without permission, hate phones, hate loud noises and crowds. These behaviors have been trained into me… they are learned behaviors that I have practiced and struggled with. They are now habit and inherent to my personality.

Additionally, I do not believe a cure for Autistic Spectrum

Disorders would result in a cure for the comorbid conditions so many Autistic Spectrum individuals suffer from along with their Autism. That means that, regardless of Autism, many Autistic Spectrum individuals are still pretty messed up people.

Also, MANY people on the spectrum do not consider themselves to have any problems. They view their Autism as a difference… not a problem. Some even consider it a gift. These people, due to the stress and anxiety associated with a major paradigm shift like this would be terribly resistant to anything of the kind.

Personally… I wouldn't do it. While my Asperger's Syndrome has caused my a lot of pain over the years. I would not trade it for anything. I have learned how to cope and am functional. I have my art and interests… and I have my habits. I wouldn't want to have to learn all these things over… And… well… my pain makes me who I am – a compassionate and thoughtful person concerned with the thoughts and feelings of others.

So… To cure or not to cure… the unborn, definitely… but the rest of us… well… it should be considered on an individual basis. Each Autistic Spectrum individual would need to make their own decisions.

Supplemental – I am what I am… And that will NOT change

The following is an open letter to the world. I write this as an Autism Self Advocate… I write this as an Autistic Spectrum individual… I write this as a self proclaimed champion of the rights and perceptions of other Autistic Spectrum individuals.

Unlike Autism Speaks, I do not claim to be THE authority on Autistic Spectrum Disorders… or even AN authority. I am just a guy who has lived through it. I am just a guy who was diagnosed with Asperger's Syndrome. I do, however, bring with me the perceptions of a mind locked into the thought patterns of an Autistic mind.

Since I write more than the basic happenings of my life… I am in a unique position.

I don't LIKE politics. At all. I don't like politicians. At all… However, because I speak out on Autistic Spectrum issues; because I seek to explain the Autistic Spectrum condition in a way that Neurotypicals can understand – I come under scrutiny that most of us do not. Perhaps because I was raised correctly… or perhaps, it is because Aspies tend to be very much aware of that which is fair and just… I can't help but do it.

If it weren't for this odd part of my personality, I would gladly write fan fiction. I would sit back and blend with the wood work and be nothing more than a quiet unassuming Aspie that people could say nothing specific about… Well, except for the fact that I am 6'9″, have an odd gray eye color, and often have dazzlingly colored hair. Instead, I have to do it.

Because Autism is a hot-button topic, and because I speak out – I KNOW that everything that I do is political in nature. Every word I write, or say… is political.

"The trouble is that once you see it, you can't unsee it. And once you've seen it, keeping quiet, saying nothing, becomes as political an act as speaking out. There is no innocence. Either way, you're accountable." ~Arundhati Roy

I can choose to pretend it's not and be an accessory to oppression… of Autistics, women, the poor, racial minorities and religious denominations… OR… I can run with it. I can take the energy of my very presence and destroy the shackles of oppression.

I have an advantage over many others that seek to do the same thing. I have Asperger's Syndrome. By the very nature of my miswired brain, I am not restricted in the same manner as others. I am not bound by the social stigmata and restrictions that Neurotypicals are.

NTs will sit in the embrace of the Status Quo and say nothing when dissatisfied. It's unseemly to rock the boat. It's rude to point out the foibles and faults of the system, other people and society. It's bad form to rail against the unjust and unfair nature of life.

As an Aspie… I get to say the things that others don't. I don't have to stick to those same rules. I can break them. I can scream to the four winds that our rape culture needs to stop; that racism is just ridiculous in this day and age; that feminism only perpetuates an us vs. them mentality and we need to invest in personism; that YOUR religion is YOUR choice and no one else's. I get to be obnoxious… it's part of the disorder.

And I will use it. I will tell you what you NEED to hear WHETHER OR NOT YOU WANT TO HEAR THEM. I will scream at the government. I will rail against the greed and corruption of the rich. I will speak my mind about the hacker that uncovered the activities of RAPISTS being sentenced to 10 years while the rapists only get two years.

I am annoying, obnoxious and unfit for civilized society because I REFUSE to be silent in the face of injustice.

If I stand by while injustice happens, i suffer all of the traditional symptoms of anxiety: trembling, blood pressure spikes, roiling stomach and difficulty breathing.

When it happens… I ACT. I don't think about it… My body and mouth moves. I don't know if this is a function of upbringing, my own experiences with injustice directed at me or the Asperger's.

My definition of injustice will probably be the same as yours. My definition is a great deal broader than most people's… I can't stand by silently… no… I REFUSE to stand by silently when you make a racist joke or use a racist slur… I REFUSE to stand by while you make a gay joke… and may the divine have mercy on you if you make a rape joke or a joke about someone who is handicapped.

I am Aspie… and you WILL hear me roar… I can't stand there and pretend that you didn't just say what you said or didn't do what you did… I won't ignore it like your NT friends and then jump back into the conversation after it has passed like nothing happened. You said it… and I will call you on it. The stupid things that you say or do… WILL be brought to your attention and the attention of those around you. I will embarrass you… I will humiliate you and make you regret your attitudes… I will shove those words back past your teeth and straight down your throat.

When I climb up your ass because you said something disparaging about a minority, a religion, sexual orientation, a disability… Remember that there is no backspace key for the spoken word and you have been lucky to live your life without repercussions for as long as you have… Remember that I am karma jumping on you and calling you on your HATE SPEECH… and that is what it is.

You say, "But that's not acceptable by societal standards!"

Guess what? I am Aspie… I am not really a part of your society… No one ever asked me to sign your social contract… So, suck it up buttercup.

And frankly…I don't want to be part of your society. We live in a culture of oppression and abuse… there is an epidemic of violent crime and rape. I can't sit down with you and have a polite conversation with you because there is NOTHING polite, civil or even RIGHT about your culture…

Here's a secret for you… I do not disagree with your intellectual acceptance of the status quo. I am physiologically UNABLE to tolerate it. I am appalled, disgusted and ENRAGED by some of the things I witness and hear.

I want to scream and rant and rave. I want to weep and roll up in a ball and flee the reality of the world because it is a society of labels, negation and callous fuckwittage…

"Once you label me you negate me."
~Søren Kierkegaard

If you can't deal with the fact that your society upsets me to the point of rage, stimming and sometimes becoming non-verbal… that's tough. I'm NOT going away. Change your society… love thy neighbor, take care of the poor, stop condoning rape and blaming the victims, stop the hate, stop the oppression, oppose corruption in the financial quarter, oppose corruption in politics and stop the violence.

Yes, I am loud, obnoxious, annoying and strident in my beliefs… because I believe in justice, sincerity, truth, compassion and (yes, dammit) the American way… the American way that I believe in, however, no longer exists… the state of this world would make Kal-el (Superman) cry… and it does the same for me.

Get used to it. You will be hearing my voice right up til the last second – right up til the mother ship calls us all home. And when that happens, enjoy that silence while you can… because you're the next target.

Do not go gentle into that good night
~by Dylan Thomas

Do not go gentle into that good night,
Old age should burn and rave at close of day;
Rage, rage against the dying of the light.

Though wise men at their end know dark is right,
Because their words had forked no lightning they
Do not go gentle into that good night.

Good men, the last wave by, crying how bright
Their frail deeds might have danced in a green bay,
Rage, rage against the dying of the light.

Wild men who caught and sang the sun in flight,
And learn, too late, they grieved it on its way,
Do not go gentle into that good night.

Grave men, near death, who see with blinding sight
Blind eyes could blaze like meteors and be gay,

Rage, rage against the dying of the light.

And you, my father, there on the sad height,
Curse, bless, me now with your fierce tears, I pray.
Do not go gentle into that good night.
Rage, rage against the dying of the light.

20 – What IS neurotypical, anyway?

The following is a piece of satire and is intended to be read as such.

I have spent a lot of time researching my condition in an effort to understand what is really going on with my life. Almost every book I have read on the subject of Autism, Asperger's Syndrome or Autism Spectrum disorders has started out with a chapter titled: "What is Autism", "What is Asperger's Syndrome" or "What is an Autistic Spectrum Disorder?"

Awesome… Let's define it… Ironically enough, none of these introductory chapters has ever gotten it right. I have gotten to the point where I skip these chapters as they are pretty much meaningless… I have the diagnostic criteria seared into my brain.

[The following is from Diagnostic and Statistical Manual of Mental Disorders: DSM IV]
Diagnostic Criteria for 299.80 Asperger's Disorder
  I. Qualitative impairment in social interaction, as manifested by at least two of the following:
      a) A. marked impairments in the use of multiple nonverbal behaviors such as eye-to-eye gaze, facial expression, body posture, and gestures to regulate social interaction
      b) failure to develop peer relationships appropriate to developmental level
      c) a lack of spontaneous seeking to share enjoyment, interest or achievements with other people, (e.g.. by a lack of showing, bringing, or pointing out objects of interest to other people)
      d) lack of social or emotional reciprocity
  II. Restricted repetitive & stereotyped patterns of behavior, interests and activities, as manifested by at least one of

the following:
  a) encompassing preoccupation with one or more
     stereotyped and restricted patterns of interest that is
     abnormal either in intensity or focus
  b) apparently inflexible adherence to specific,
     nonfunctional routines or rituals
  c) stereotyped and repetitive motor mannerisms (e.g.
     hand or finger flapping or twisting, or complex
     whole-body movements)
  d) persistent preoccupation with parts of objects
III. The disturbance causes clinically significant
     impairments in social, occupational, or other important
     areas of functioning.
IV. There is no clinically significant general delay in
     language (E.G. single words used by age 2 years,
     communicative phrases used by age 3 years)
V. There is no clinically significant delay in cognitive
     development or in the development of age-appropriate
     self help skills, adaptive behavior (other than in social
     interaction) and curiosity about the environment in
     childhood.
VI. Criteria are not met for another specific Pervasive
     Developmental Disorder or Schizophrenia."

I ask you… How often do you see THAT in the first chapter?
Never… Not once… Well… I did ONCE, but that was a manual
for mental health professionals. But never will you see any
beginner's guide, parent's guide, idiot's guide or book geared to
the public that will do anything more than spout comforting
fluff and emotional platitudes about how it gets better.

THAT.
IS.
WRONG.

Seriously… It's just wrong.

It doesn't get better… It doesn't get easier. If anything, as the Autistic mine develops, it gets harder. Take the terrible twos, and add Autism. Take the teenage years, and add Autism. Take 18 and add Autism. Take school, bullies, love, hormones and the difficulties of becoming a social creature… and add Autism.

So… the first chapter of this book should really be "What is Neurotypical?"

Neurotypical is a term that gets bandied about any Autism website, community or meetup. They throw it out there like everyone should know what it means… on an instinctive level. This is probably a new word for you, even if you've been reading this series. The word is used, sometimes in a derogatory manner, to refer to people who are not on the Autistic Spectrum. It's a mish-mash of the words "neurologically typical." We often shorten it to the abbreviation "NT."

Originally, it was used to refer to someone NOT on the Autistic Spectrum. It has evolved to cover anyone who doesn't have atypical neurology. In other words – it is: anyone who is not Autistic, Dyslexic, Dysporaxic, Bipolar, or ADD/ADHD. Recently, some have pushed for the term "Allistic," which has the same meaning as neurotypical. The concept has been embraced widely by the Neurodiversity movement and the Scientific Community. Technically, you can be allistic and still be neurotically, even if you aren't autistic.

How can we tell if someone is Neurotypical? I mean, who are these NTs… how can you tell if someone in your family might have the dreaded condition referred to as Neurotypicality?

First off, it is very likely that one of your family, or someone close to you is an NT. They make up 99% of the population. This means that, LITERALLY, they are everywhere. It is

EXTREMELY likely that you know NTs and you almost
certainly have one in your family.

While no diagnostic test exists for the NT condition, it is
fairly easy to spot one… Once you know you are looking for.
Keep in mind however, these are sweeping generalizations.
ALL NTs, just like Aspies, are different.

Inability or Unwillingness to Take Words at Face Value

Due to the nature of NT society and communication, they
have been trained to accept the fact that everyone they
encounter will wear these masks. Therefore, when you tell
them, "Due to the fact that I will have Asperger's, I will
probably offend you." They cannot accept it. When you tell
them that, "I meant what I said, nothing more, nothing less."
They cannot accept it. If you hear the question, "What did you
mean by that?" and it was not a complex mathematical,
linguistic, physics, cosmological or quantum mechanics
concept, they are probably NT. Move on, no matter how many
times you say, "I meant exactly what I said," they will not
believe you. If you attempt to clarify by asking which word was
the one that they need help with and they get offended, they are
probably an NT.

Touching

NTs like to touch. They enjoy all sorts of intense, casual,
inappropriate and uncomfortable touching. This physical
contact is used to greet, identify, groom, and dominate. They are
a bit like infants in that way – they experience the world
through their sense of touch. It may be odd to be hugged by
someone that you don't know, but roll with it. Remember, they
can't help it. They are simply wired differently than you and I.

Double Speak or Confusing Communication

NTs are trained from birth to wear masks. To be true to one's
self is considered uncouth or rude. As such, NT communication

can be a frustrating minefield. Try putting together an outfit that you KNOW looks horrible. Then go ask some NTs what they think. If they are not familiar with your condition, they will, without a doubt, tell you how great it looks on you. They are so mired down by the concepts of politeness and kindness to others that they are completely and utterly unable to give a straight answer without years of training in Aspie-NT communications. As such, while wearing this outfit, you will be able to identify them by their commentary of "Looking good!"

Chatting

The most telling trait of NTs is their desire to chat or make small talk. In spite of the seeming meaninglessness of small talk, it serves a VERY specific purpose to the NT brain. It is a repetitive ritual for them that eases them into the depths of social interaction. If you TRULY want to make an NT comfortable – it is best to humor them and participate in this ritual to the limits of your tolerance. With time and patience, it is possible to lure your NT into a sense of comfort. Once they are in this level of comfort, they will possibly move from chatting into in depth and comfortable conversation.

But what IS Neurotypical. It is a flawed wiring of the brain and the mechanisms of neural function that leads a person to be or desire many of the following.
- normal – and if they are not normal, an intense desire to be so.
- Fashionable
- one of the "in crowd"
- popular
- thought well of
- rich
- famous
- surrounded by friends
- like bars

- like concerts
- like the mall
- like music festivals
- like crowds
- have no volume control
- engage in social mask wearing
- middle of the road, part of the status quo.

The NT mind is one that is saddled with the simian instincts to be a group creature. Studies of group dynamics have shown that they are, with a few notable exceptions, unable to engage in truly individual behavior until prompted to do so by an outside stimulus or another person in their community group. (The words community group engender an extremely fluid concept that literally changes from moment to moment).

As studies have shown, the NT mind is unable to process all of the information thrown at it, allowing them to process a PORTION of the data that they experience and are immersed in.

Take a moment to watch this video: https://youtu.be/oSQJP40PcGI

As this video demonstrates, they are unable to process the full imagery of a simple 640×480 video. Imagine how much information must be discarded for them to take in the world around them. While information overload can dazzle the Aspie senses, can you imagine what it is like to be restricted to such a minuscule trickle of information.

Imagine the emotional and mental drain of the masks they wear. To have to CONSTANTLY animate muscles that are weak on tone must be exhausting. Further, to be plagued by a constant series of "Micro expressions" seems horrible to me… I cannot imagine the weakness one must feel to have the emotional impact of everything said, every event and thought play out across their face.

The lack of hyper-focus and special interests must be an emotional suck hole as well. Imagine, if you can, the ability to become… bored. The lack of constant cycling, thought and joy that a special interest brings. Imagine having to search for something to do. Imagine having to involve others just so your mind didn't idle – urging you to do something… ANYTHING… imagine having to imbibe alcohol to shut it off.

All of this, and more, is what it is like to be an NT. It sound horrible, and I am sure it is. But we need to remember something when dealing with the NTs in our lives. They can't help it. They are wired differently than us, and while they envy many of our traits, they are doing the best they can. They need the same love and compassion that we all need and crave.

So, be kind to your NT. They are a special flower in your garden. If you can see past their neurological differences, you can foster a potent and rewarding relation ship for yourself… And them.

I know I have been making a big deal about how difficult having an Aspie in your life can be… And I've caught a bit of heat for it. The point of it has been to give you an honest and open appraisal of who and what we are. And I know… we're all different people. That's why there is so much to cover in this series.

As one of my readers pointed out, sometimes it can come across as "Us vs. Them" and at one point made a comment comparing it to the invasion of Poland.

So… I'm going to say the things that have not been said… that I probably should have. Yes… it can be a huge pain in the ass to have an Aspie in your life. We can be rude, confusing, standoffish, angry, embarrassing and sometimes, childish. If you can get past all that, you will discover something… There is no person better suited to be a friend to you, to tell you the things you want to hear, to be the ultimate support structure. Aspies (on the whole) are funny, creative, intelligent and FIERCELY devoted to those that make the effort. We have problems making friends… so when we FINALLY do get someone into that "ZONE". That person is a friend for LIFE… I am serious here.

Let's just look at my friendships… There is the Business Partner – 6 years of active interactive friendship. P.K.S. – 20 years… YES… 20 years. Shade – Her mate and my best friend – 20 years. The fluffy one – 22 years. Suavo – 18 years. The Bean – 17 years. I think you can see the trend here… God, I hope you can see the trend, cause that's them. I have others, but they are newer relationships.

So, if you can foster a relationship with your Aspie, even if they never say anything about it, even if they don't express how much they appreciate it… you have entered into an intense and beautiful relations.

But, it's not fair to you to let you come into this crossfire unprepared. You can see why I want to be fair, right? If I outline the problems you MIGHT encounter and paint them in the worse light possible… when you get to that hurdle, you can say… that wasn't so bad, was it?

Speaking of fairness… I know, Holy Segue, Batman! We tend to have a very black and white view of things. This is part of how we are wired. This leads to a very strong sense of right and wrong… or more specifically, fair and unfair. And the Aspie may not know that is what this specific mechanism is manifesting as, and may use the terms right and wrong instead.

You may find yourself on the wrong end of Aspie outrage due to something they have witnessed or an event out in the world. Things like people bashing a tennis player because of the fact that she is not an amazonian goddess, but she still won (story here); the reactions IN FAVOR of this asshat (story here); states infringing on gay rights in SPITE of the laws protecting it (story here); the choices that businessmen have to make due to the new healthcare laws (story here); these asshats (story here); or something as simple as the way people treat their servers at restaurants (stories here). Hell, even something as simple and commonplace as a line jumper at your local grocery store can invoke that sense of fair play, make your Aspie angry and can completely ruin their day due to the anxiety, outrage and (yes) even rage at this violation of right and wrong.

And honestly, your Aspie may be exposed to these things and not even know what has upset them. I know that I've been there, personally. They experience something that is unfair, whether it be to them or to another, and it doesn't sit right… This can and, often, does cause cognitive dissonance… And as we've discussed in the past, unresolved cognitive dissonance will feed back on itself.

You are out of balance due to dissonance, which makes you question why you are dissonant (why do I feel this way?) and the nature of cognitive dissonance is such that once it is invoked in the Aspie mind, we may not be able to see back to the beginning and all we can do is wail, "I don't know!!! I am just… upset!"

As a result of this, the unconscious mind (such as it is in Aspies – which is a topic for another day), will develop a defense mechanism. After being exposed to unfairness, then developing into a full blown dissonant loop event (patent pending on that term) a couple times, the brain finds work arounds for the resulting chaos and systemic problems caused by these events.

Unfortunately for those around us, the Aspie brain takes the most expedient route in most cases… i.e. When confronted by unfairness, we confront it… head on… when pushed, we push back.

In physiological terms, this means that the Aspie will become agitated and angry. These emotions stimulate different parts of the brain allowing function to be shunted to a different processing center, bypassing the dissonant areas of the brain and allowing the offending stimuli to be removed in an efficient and expedient manner.

In practical terms, this means that your Aspie is going to react. The severity of the reaction is dependent on the severity of the infraction. A line jumper is going to be called out, right there in front of everyone for his rude behavior. A sexist remark or joke is going to result in the commenter being advised (in no uncertain terms) that their behavior is inappropriate.

The following is an example from my life and is considered intensely personal. This was 7 days after the terrorist attacks on the World Trade Center (9/11). I was a college student at the University of Missouri (Columbia). I am walking to class and I look to my left and there are six or seven Caucasian men in a semicircle against the wall, yelling at something. I walk over to see what is going on. There is a small middle eastern (actually Indian) man on the ground with a bloody nose. He has curled into the fetal position and is weeping.

*The men are standing over him, yelling… (I know, I said that already.) They are saying a lot of racist things to this poor man. I can only two of the comments. "Go back where you came from, towel head ***Expletive deleted***" and "We're going to punish you for all those people you ***expletive deleted** killed."*

There was no other option… this was not fair. Not only was the man at risk for his life, but it was for something that he had no connections to. (I swear, Americans have no cultural awareness, or eye for physical differences between cultures) I was outraged… in the extreme. Cognitive dissonance started, but was shorted out and cut off by the rage reflex, preventing a dissonant loop and (as my friends call it) brain vapor lock. Instead of witnessing, I acted.

I stepped into their semicircle and said… Said is a misnomer… I bellowed… "Hey! Why don't you pick on someone MY size." Let me paint you a picture here… I am 6'9" (yes, almost 7 feet tall and that is Over 2 meters tall for my metric friends). I weighed in at 220 pounds (99.8 kg). I have shoulder length flamingo pink hair at this point… Combat boots, leather jacket, chain on the shoulder, wallet chain, etc… I am sure that when the Pink Crested Weirdo stepped up and presented (a naturist term for aggressive stances in wild animals used to either intimidate a rival or attract a mate)… they were taken aback. There was still violent action, I was cut and bruised, but it was the right thing, the fair thing to do.

"Pick on someone MY SIZE!"

This is, I admit, an extreme case… but think about this… In every situation, since Aspies do not have the shades of gray required for a polite resolution to these situations. As such, when confronted with something so far out of the realm of right or wrong (i.e. fair or unfair), they are going to react in the extreme ways that they feel the witnessed behavior warrants.

Often, this will come completely out of left field. You will be having a good day, and BANG!, your Aspie is on a tear.

However, this can also make you realize how precious your Aspie is to the world.

This is another example from my own life. The Bean and I were eating at a buffet. There was an older couple talking about the summer camp they run for disadvantaged youth. Everything in the camp is run by volunteers, no one takes home any pay. It gives these children a chance to do something other than sit at home, alone, all summer while their parents work.

The cost per child to the organization running the camp was $50 a child. They were short that summer, and were likely going to have to turn away several children.

This wasn't fair. There were good children that needed this program. I knew from personal experience that a summer of heat so stifling that they had to stay indoors and be bored was miserable.
I happened to have an extra $50 in my pocket. So I gave it to them.

We are capable of what others will consider kindness… but it is only in the interests of fairness and equality.

Don't be shocked if something in the media or their life causes your Aspie outrage. We are often told that we are over-reacting. And perhaps that is true, but I believe that some over-reaction is necessary. Perhaps if people reacted, or better ACTED to prevent the injustices in the world, Aspies wouldn't have to OVER-react. Pay attention to their distress in these issues, and you might be outraged, too.

Dating can be difficult for your Aspie for a number of reasons. Most of them, at least by my reckoning, are because of the expectations, perceptions and expectations of Neurotypicals. The reason this part doesn't mention dating in the title is that this extends beyond the realm of dating and into many social situations as well.

Let's start with clothes. Aspies wear clothes that they like. Most of the time these consist of comfortable articles, often made from cloth that is soft to the touch. As an example, my wardrobe consists of military BDU style pants (in black and gray). They are made from ripstop (explained here) because durability is a factor. I have many VERY comfortable t-shirts and those are augmented by a lot of bowling shirts worn as over shirts.

That is it. Well, that's not true. I have a tuxedo.

Recently I met someone in public. I was advised that my appearance was a huge "turn off" for her. When I pushed for more information, it was my clothes…

She wore jeans, a t-shirt, and Chinese style slippers. I wore my black pants, a gray t-shirt and my nice limited edition chuck tailors. Intrinsically, we were dressed very similar. However, it was interpreted as I made no effort.

I asked her for input, and it came out that she thought my shirt was too small. (nowhere on my body was it tight, the shoulder seems sit where they are supposed to) side note: I did not tuck it in as I have been advised that this is the fashion. She stated that my pants were too big… which is odd, because they barely fit, I popped the button off that pair recently, and they are too short… That I looked sloppy. My hair, which has cowlicks, had no product in it. I don't wear product, it is sticky and when I sweat (I live in New Orleans, I WILL sweat) it runs down my face, gets in my eyes and down my shirt. My hair was wet… because, I was sweating. And I wasn't wearing cologne. I don't own cologne because of sensory issues… all but the most expensive colognes stink to me.

So… basically, she was stating that I dress and look like what I am, an Aspie. In a previous part of this series I said, "Don't try to emulate NT fashion… this is a recipe for failure. If you do, expect to be a meme of some sort." This event drove this concept home.

All of my choices boiled down to me being told that it was "Sloppy."

I was frustrated and hurt… not because she would say that, but because this was probably a true statement coming from an NT… Which is an oddity. In the course of normal conversations, NTs will attempt to be nice and spare your feelings which results in many confusing statements, none of which get to the point. Here she was – completely blunt about it.

So… You have probably noticed that your Aspie dresses like an Aspie… that is to say, comfortable, sometimes silly, clothes. Unless they were one of the rare .01% that was actually "cool" in their school career, chances are they are inherently and painfully aware that their clothing is… odd… More than one of us has been chided with a variant of "You dress like an autistic."

And you know what? That's fine… It is more than fine… It is who we are.

NT social expectations are such that we have to make an effort in the social arena. If you are meeting with someone you like, you have to make an effort. We do. If your Aspie is shower fresh, in clean clothes and meeting you somewhere outside of their comfort zone (i.e. not someplace they usually hang out) they are making a MONUMENTAL effort.

The NT in question was offended, her feelings were hurt because my effort did not show in a way she could understand.

Your Aspie will do many things to please you. They will bend over backwards to make you feel good, but there are things they just can't do.

What most Aspies can't grasp is clothes don't make you cool. You can dress us up, but we won't be cool… and if the clothes are not comfortable or not what we feel comfortable in, we will be a few degrees off, no matter what we do.

From the Aspie view point, this is one of those points that just needs to be accepted. Our way of dress is not at all, in any way, a reflection of our feelings, intent, or respect for the people around us. NTs need to understand that what you see as sloppy is simply comfortable for us.

23 – Information Processing and Autistic Spectrum Individuals

When psychiatrists discuss behavior, they refer to "models". There have been numerous models used to describe the behaviors associated with autism in the years since scientists accepted that there is a neurological basis for the condition. While none of them have completely described the Autistic condition, they have made significant inroads in understanding the characterization and cognitive basis for Autism. The current understanding has it explained as a series of cognitive deficits and a complex disorder in information processing.

A recent study in the UK suggests what Autistic Spectrum individuals have been saying amongst themselves for years – we are capable of processing VAST amounts of information… Often much more than Neurotypicals. The study presented information rapidly, and Autistic Spectrum individuals were able to process the information much more rapidly than NTs. It also states that Autistic Spectrum individuals were better at detecting "critical" information. (I'm not sure what that means, but it sounds scientific).

There is a higher than average concentration of Autistic Spectrum individuals in the IT industry, and the researchers feel that the results of this study help explain this. While this information is true… I believe it is far more likely that the reason for this is that the average IT job allows the Autistic Spectrum individual (I am toying with the word Autist to simplify this concept and compliment the term Allist) the freedom to work with little in the way of outside distraction. With most IT positions being managed by a ticket system, complaints are logged into a system and assigned to IT professionals, there is very little interaction with the public needed. Further, computers act and react in predictable ways, allowing the Autist to problem solve in a logical and progressive manner.

As you know, Autistic Spectrum Disorders are a class of lifelong developmental disorders that affect social interaction and communication. Studies have shown that Autists have an increased ability to focus (hyper-focus) on certain tasks benefiting from a greater attention span and ability to process information on those tasks.

The problem with this is that, while we are able to process information in a more efficient manner than NTs, we can become easily distracted. If the subject matter is not interesting to us, if there is a lot of outside stimuli in our work area, if there are a lot of irrelevant data in the information to be processed, if the information is presented in a disorderly or efficient way, or if there is a kitty – we can be come distracted easily.

Professor Nilli Lavie of the University College of London hypothesized something that I have stated for years: the combination of hyper-focus and distractibility (It's a word… I may have made it up, but distractibility is soooo a word… Use it…pass it around… get it into common parlance… let's get it in the dictionary!) is a result of the Autist's brain to process a higher volume of information than that of an NT. (I'm just coining new words left and right tonight!).

"Our work on perceptual capacity in the typical adult brain suggests a clear explanation for the unique cognitive profile that people with autism show," she says. *"People who have higher perceptual capacity are able to process more information from a scene, but this may also include some irrelevant information which they may find harder to ignore. Our research suggests autism does not involve a distractibility deficit but rather an information processing advantage."*

Before I continue, it has been pointed out that Nillie Lavie used distractibility… So… I copyrighted it… and great minds think alike… use it… pass it around… let's get it in the dictionary!

The scientists conducted their study on 32 adults. Half of these were NTs. The other half were Autistic Spectrum individuals. They put a circle of letters that flashed briefly on the screen while the test subjects were asked to look for specific letters while at the same time tasked with detecting a small gray shape that that popped up from time to time outside of the circle.

While there were only one or two letters on the screen, NTs and Autists performed comparably. As the difficulty of the task increased (the speed and number of letters increased), the NTs experienced a deterioration of their ability to detect the shape and "target" letters. The Autists, on the other hand, did not experience the same difficulty. As the task became more difficult, the Autistic Spectrum individuals consistently outperformed the NTs.

Lavie goes on to say that whether or not an Autist has the savant like abilities of Kim Peek (Wiki article here) or Stephen Wiltshire (site here), her study seems to indicate that this higher perceptual threshold is a trait that most Autists would seem to share.

I don't know if I can explain it very well, but I will try. I have discussed this whole topic with many NTs and discovered some differences between us. According to my pet NTs and several scientific papers I have read… the average person perceives a fraction of what they see. (numbers range from as low as 4% to as high as 60%) As an example, please look at the following image.

I have been assured that NTs can read this information pretty easily. I managed to decipher it after a bit of work. According to this graphic (and every NT I know) the first and last letter being in the proper place renders the word jumbles completely intelligible.

I have presented this same graphic to several Autistic Spectrum individuals and after their head exploded, we cleaned the walls and put the bits back together, we sat down and took a good long look at it. Since we possess the vocabulary for it, and the first and last letters are already in place, solving the anagrams was relatively easy… but because my brain takes in the entire word for processing, there was no instant understanding or even understanding at a glance.

I posted a variant of this video in a previous part of this series, but this one is unique. Take a look.
https://youtu.be/IGQmdoK_ZfY

I caught it… and most of the Autistic Spectrum individuals caught it, too…

The NT brain buffers itself by only allowing perceptive retention (patent pending, again) of only a small fraction of what it sees. And honestly, that is all that is needed for human survival. We don't need to see the grass in every nerve impulse… once it's been seen, it is cataloged and indexed and then the brain moves on, filtering every thing that is non-essential out. There's cars over there, grass here, DOG! Oh, he's just playing Frisbee… This constant filtering is both a great strength in NT perceptual cognition and a flaw, as things can easily be overlooked.

On the other side of the coin is the Autistic Spectrum brain. Each nerve impulse takes in everything within visual range without filtering. We don't stop seeing or noticing the cars… We're probably counting them. We don't stop seeing the grass… The dog, since it is pleasing to the eye, moves with a grace that humans are not capable of and has fur – stays in our perceptive cognition.

We see a great deal more than the NTs around us… As with the NT brain however, this is both a strength and a weakness. We notice many more details and can process an amazing amount of information… for a while. Then we become over-stimulated.

I have had several NTs tell me that they cannot wrap their minds around the concept of over-stimulation. I came up with a simple way to demonstrate it. Gently scratch your arm, moving only your fingers. They will cross the same spot over and over again. Don't stop scratching. DO NOT vary tempo or pressure. Keep doing it. Keep going… now stop. While you have not damaged your skin, it feels irritated and raw. In spite of the fact that this is not the case.

That's what over stimulation is. It isn't what it is like… you have just overstimulated the nerves in that small patch of skin. Now… take that sensation and imagine what it would be like to see too much… so that your optic nerve was over stimulated… or to smell to much… taste, or hear too much. Difficult to wrap your mind around, isn't it? While it happens to us on a regular basis, it is no easier to explain than it is to understand.

So… while I have been told by a couple NTs that they envy my perceptual acuity, i envy them the ability to go to a party, concert or a bar without just overloading.

24 – Parents of Autists and Socialization

Parents of Autists (Autistic Spectrum individuals) want the best for their children. On of the biggest issues for Autists is socialization. The inability of their child to socialize in any meaningful way breaks many parent's hearts. Parents will often seek to foster interpersonal relationships.

There are some common approaches that many parents take in this situation.

The following statements are blanket statements and there may be exceptions. If there are exceptions, revel in them.

Play dates
They will make play dates with children from their child's class. Unless your child is in a special education class specifically for Autists, this is probably not going to work. Your Autistic Spectrum child is having problems with social skills. This means that they are having problems socializing with that group of children. Even if the class is unaware of the Autistic nature of your child is not common knowledge, the children in their class will sense that there is something different about them.

When we come right down to it… we are primates. Primates are social animals. In nature, differences, are often punished… by shunning, violence and even death. Differences, on an instinctual level, mean that another animal is unwell, of a different species, old or infirm. As we evolved into a civilized animal, we put the violent actions aside (for the most part), but kept our desire to avoid those that are different and seek out those that are like us.

So, your Autist child will have the same problems with these play dates as they do in class. Forcing them to associate with a child that senses these differences will only make them uncomfortable. As we have previously discussed, discomfort can lead to anxiety, cognitive dissonance or worse.

Group Activities

Sometimes, parents will attempt to solve the socialization problem by encouraging their child to engage in group activities. This can be camp, boy scouts, girl scouts, church youth group, sports, the park… anything of the sort.

We're already discussed the instinctual responses of the other children, so I will not go back over that.

Let's look at it from the Autist's standpoint. Assuming there are no sensory issues… what we see is a swirl of children moving around, all of them able to instinctively interacting. They walk up, look at each other, read body language, micro-expressions and can (pretty much) instantly decide whether or not they want to play together.

We can't do that… it puts things into a harsh light. Even if we do not have the cognitive capacity to comprehend what is happening, but we know… we know we are different. We are acutely aware that we are not the same. It is uncomfortable, unsettling and can be soul crushing.

What's worse is when another child wants to play with us. Because we've (in most cases) never really experienced it, we are unsure… Some of us have actually been bullied or emotionally abused enough that we are suspicious of the motives of anyone that wants to spend time with us and we may not be able to accept their motives as pure. In retrospect… in my own childhood, I missed many opportunities that could have led to beautiful friendships… all because I was unable to accept their overtures as pure.

In all likelihood, there are sensory issues on top of the social issues… which complicates things even more.

Autist Support Groups

To many parents, this seems like an ideal solution. A group of parents that understand, or at the least, can empathize with your situation. A group of Autists that can be friends… On the surface, it seems to be perfect. For the parents, it can be… but for the children it can be a nightmare.

How can this be, you ask? Well… Let's look at it from a Neurotypical standpoint.

I suggest this thought experiment. Assume that someone else is responsible for providing you with a social circle to interact with.

They look at you and try to predict who you would like to interact with.

They try putting you in a group with your own gender… Boys like playing with boys, right? Girls like playing with girls… isn't that right?

So… that didn't work… what else is there… Let's try other combinations… You have long hair – they have long hair. You like music – they like music. You wear shoes – they wear shoes.

This is a simplification of a complex idea. Essentially, this is what you are doing. You are saying, "You have Asperger's Syndrome… They have Asperger's Syndrome… You should be friends."

Parents will often assume that the presence of Autism Spectrum Disorders is enough to forge a friendship with… This is patently false. Can you jump into a group of people and forge a friendship with all of them? Hell, even most of them? No. You are picky about who your friends are, and they have to have at least something in common with you. The fact that you are Neurotypical and they are Neurotypical is not enough to build a friendship with… is it?

I have been to one of these meet ups. Aspies all have Special Interests. Unless a pair of Aspies share one or more of their Special Interests, they really have nothing on common… Aside from being an Autist… and this is not enough to make a friendship out of.

Recently, I started speaking with another Autist who uses the name "Shadro". She and I share a special interest – Photography. We have a great deal in common and are on the way to (I feel) becoming friends. We've spent the last few days sharing nerd-gasms over lenses and cameras and comparing notes on l series vs m series lenses, 7d versus t3i, prime lenses versus zoom lenses… But this is a rarity.

When an Aspie discovers a Special Interest (whether it is a short term or lifelong one), we research all that we can. There are differences in cognitive capabilities, available research materials, personal experiences, anecdotal research from third party sources… As such, each Aspie can, within a short time, be considered an authority in the bailiwick of their Special Interest.

They can be considered an Authority, and whether or not they express it in that manner, they KNOW that they know more than those around them about it.

Often, however, each Aspie will take different things away from the research and experience than the others. This can, and often does, lead to Aspies with the same Special Interest at cross purposes. Since one will insist that their method, understanding and experience led them to conclusion A and the other will insist that the same things have led them to conclusion B, it can get difficult.

Aspies don't see things in shades of gray. It is black and white. If a thing is true, then it is right. If a thing is true, then the other way must be wrong. While this is an incorrect logical conclusion, it is almost ingrained into the way we think. As a spectrum – the higher the cognitive capabilities of the Aspie, the more able the Aspie is to accept a specific way, thought or pattern, or concept may not be the only way.

Unfortunately, since both are so ADDICTED to the information they posses... since they have FOUGHT to acquire this information... Since we have that same rush of endorphins that NTs experience when falling in love when discussing our special interests... We are passionate about it... and we KNOW what we KNOW... no one can tell us differently... It is not an intolerance of other thought patterns... it is a clash of complimentary passions...

So, even if you put two Aspies with the same special interest together, it is no guarantee that they will become friends. While it hurts your heart to see them without friends... don't force it. This only serves your own purposes, not theirs. Help them learn the social skills – how to talk to people, facial expression recognition, conversation skills, eye contact... and they will develop friendships on their own... naturally.

25 – Aspies, Pain and Perception

I have heard the Neurotypicals in my life comment on my processing and perceptions of pain. As a result, my sister (also Aspie) and I had a long conversation about Autistic perceptions, Neurotypical Perceptions and pain. We came to some interesting conclusions.

Often, you will notice some odd things about your Autist and their tolerance for pain. Sometimes, it will seem that they don't feel pain at all. Other times they will be hyper-sensitive to one form of pain and completely oblivious to others… Often in a way that is seemingly chaotic or lacking in any semblance of order.

I have heard questions like, how can my Autist not notice that they just cut themselves and are bleeding all over the place; How can my Autistic Spectrum child not even seem to care about the bruised hands and knees from a fall; but a light touch on the shoulder elicits a wince and groan of pain?

The question that one has to ask is this: Is your Aspie actually experiencing pain differently? Does he have a higher threshold for pain? Or is he just less verbally expressive of their pain?

After polling several other Aspies, as well as speaking to my sister on the subject – it seems that we don't process pain in the same way or at all. In my sister's case, she often will not realize that something is wrong until the offending body part stops functioning properly. As with all things that fall within the range of Aspie experience, it seems that pain is an all or nothing affair for us. I truly believe this statement applies to 99% of Aspies… There will be a small number that are different, but that is always the case.

How do we measure pain? At the hospital they will present

you with a chart that has a series of faces on it. This scale seems useless to me. The word moderate doesn't seem, in my paradigm to be a word that should not be applied to pain. I am either moderately inconvenienced or close to incapacitated.

Anecdotal evidence gathered from external sources has yielded stories of Aspies spraining their ankles and walking on it within 3 or 4 hours, bladder infections and kidney stones that were described as "annoying" as opposed to painful, wisdom teeth extracted with no follow up painkiller, nearly severed fingers not being noticed until the site was covered in blood and the like. From my personal experiences – I recently had two teeth extracted…no additional painkiller after the operation and only minimal discomfort.

The idea of moderate pain, is an alien concept for me and many others. The only conclusion that I can come to is that we, as Aspies, (GENERALLY) process pain differently.

Let's talk about pain that doesn't seem to make sense. These light touches and caresses that elicit a pain response, I believe (and the behavioral models seem to support this) are a result of a mechanism other than actual pain. Due to the sensory issues that are inherent to Autistic Spectrum Individuals, this pain response may be a combination of sudden exposure over-stimulation and the resulting cognitive dissonance. I can say that when I am experiencing a dissonant episode and I am aware of it, I have often explained it as "my brain feels too big for my skull" and it "hurts". I am not sure of the validity of this supposition, but I cannot help but "feel" that I am accurate.

Personally, I have a high pain threshold. The Bean, P.K.S. and Shade have described it as stoic, but that's not accurate. Once the initial trauma of injury passes, i just don't notice it. I always have small bruises from smacking my hand on doorknobs, hitting my knees on things, small cuts, accidents with a hot glue gun and the like. Often, I don't know that I've been injured til later (sometimes, much later).

From what the NTs in my life have explained to me. This is not the way THEY process pain. Small injuries can seem almost insurmountable and extremely traumatic. They will not remember from one time to the next what it felt like.

When it comes to pain, perception and processing – the main difference (aside from what I have covered thus far) is in anticipation and fear. Since we don't process the mild pains, we don't often have apprehension when facing a situation that might be painful.

Going back to my tooth extraction example: I have spoken to NTs in similar situations. They are afraid of the dentist and the pain that the procedure will cause. They are afraid to the point of being terrified. According to studies, anticipation of pain can amplify the effects of the actual pain by several orders of magnitude.

In my example, I was terrified... but not because a fear of the pain. I was terrified of the concept of someone I don't know sticking their hands in my mouth. I was terrified by the idea of being touched by a pair of people in a BRIGHT room with strange smells. I was terrified of being pinned to an uncomfortable chair by my teeth... and I was terrified of complications due to anesthetic, but not by the pain.

Yup... I was terrified.

I know an NT that had the same two teeth removed. The NT whined and complained for a couple weeks as they healed. They were restricted to soft foods and soups. The words here are not intended to cast a negative light on their experience... It is to illustrate that I have no frame of reference.

The day after I had my teeth out, I was hungry, so I went to Rallys and had a couple of their Smokin' Sausage for lunch.

So… You may need to be vigilant with your Aspie. Be on the look out for injuries that they have sustained but may not have noticed. These can, at times, be dangerous or even life threatening. Don't over-react though… just be vigilant… It is possible for your Aspie to fracture or break a bone… they can get small cuts… both of which open them up to infection… and they would not notice it until the injury has become an actual problem…

Also, be sure to listen… An expression of pain can be indicative of a dissonant event or actual damage. Either way, these expressions should be monitored and taken seriously as they are not something minor and have, instead, registered on the Aspie radar.

26 – Depression

Let's discuss Autistic Spectrum individuals and Depression. Studies have shown that Autistic Spectrum individuals suffer from depression at a higher than average rate than the mean. That is to say, there is a higher incidence of Depression in Autistic Spectrum individuals than there is in Neurotypicals. Several studies have also claimed genetic markers in common with both of the conditions.

The reason that I am discussing this is that there are a lot of misconceptions surrounding what depression really is.

I have read many people talking about how they can identify with those of us with depression, bipolar and greater depression… I try not to minimize the experiences of others, but I have to in this instance.

There is a difference between having an emotional response that is depressing and the realities of clinical depression and bi-polar disorder.

To facilitate communication in this piece, I will be using the blanket term "bi-polar" for all clinical depressive conditions and "depression" for the emotional condition. Clinical depression is not an emotional condition. While depression can accompany down cycles, it is not a given.

Simply put, depression is a reasonable response to emotional stimuli. When something sad happens, you experience depression, heal emotionally, and move on. Bi-polar is almost, but not entirely, unlike this.

Often, a bi-polar down cycle will not include the emotion of depression. It is possible, with cognitive behavioral modification (EXPLAINED HERE), for an individual to pull themselves out of a depressive episode… with bi-polar down cycles, this is not possible… at least, not without chemical intervention.

Bi-polar is an illness that involves body, thoughts and moods. There is drastic alteration in sleeping patterns, the way you think and feel about yourself and others around you, and even the way you eat. Without treatment, bi-polar down cycles can last for weeks months or years.

I could give many professional accounts or distill clinical reports to tell you what the psychiatric professionals have to say about the condition, but I think it might be better to share my own personal accounts.

Let's start by talking about manic phases. A manic episode is described as an elevated or expansive mood. That is a very minimalistic… almost ascetic way to explain it. Your self esteem balloons… not in an arrogant way, but you are certain that you can do ANYTHING you put your mind to, even if these ideas are inherently flawed. You don't need to sleep. Your ideas fly through your head like bullets out of a chain gun. You have difficulty focusing… You can't sit still. You talk fast… I mean really fast.

You feel ten feet tall and bullet proof… And here's the weird thing… YOU DON'T KNOW that you are being like that… you just feel good… too good… good, powerful, capable and energetic.

When you get into a down cycle… that all changes. I can't get out of bed. It's not that I am too depressed to get up… it's like I am sick. Have you ever had the flu and been too exhausted to even get up and pee? That's what it is like. I am an insomniac in my every day life… but when depressed, I will sleep for days on end.

I can't eat when in a cycle. Just no appetite… and forcing something down into my stomach will make me nauseous. I feel as if I am worthless… Like my films, writing, art and photography are worthless. I can't focus. Even on my favorite things… I can't edit movies. I can't play video games. I can't write… My sex drive falls off. I can't cook. The phrase, "I hate," pops into my head from time to time… completely without stimulation or reason. It just pops in there… ESPECIALLY when I am not thinking about anything else.

I know, this all sounds like depression… but I've been depressed and had bi-polar down cycles… handing a depressed person chocolate, or a puppy, or a kitten, or a soda can help for a while (until they are healed emotionally), but not with a down cycle.

There are also hypomanic phases… which are kind of like manic phases, but not quite as intense… and then there are hypermanic episodes… If being manic is being ten-foot tall and bullet-proof – a hypermanic episode feels like being Godzilla on crack… (for the record, I have never done crack, but hypermanic episodes… feel like it)…

From here on on, the term depressive represents the down cycles of bi-polar. There are further complications that can compound these issues.

Rapid cycling bi-polar:
Rapid cycling is defined as four or more manic, hypomanic, or depressive episodes in any 12-month period. While I am sure that this happens in some cases, in reality… most people that are rapid cycling (at least the ones I know) can cycle from a depressive cycle to manic multiple times in a week… or sometimes even a day. These rapid changes can make someone unpredictable at best.

Greater Depression:
Instead of being bi-polar, Greater Depression is referred to as unipolar… This means that someone will have down cycles without ever experiencing the euphoric, unreal, super-manisms of a manic, hypomanic or hypermanic phases. They will go from normal to… bleh… and stay there sometimes…

Then… there is

MIXED Bi-polar:
Imagine if you will… being able to have both a depressive episode and a manic, hypomanic or hypermanic episode simultaneously… A mixed bi-polar individual will be both depressive and manic at the same time. I should re-word that… Try to simply wrap your mind around that concept. I can guarantee that, if you aren't mixed bi-polar, there is no way that you can actually imagine it. Needless to say, it sucks.

So, if your Aspie is one of those unfortunates that are afflicted with some form of depressive or bipolar disorder, they may need some additional understanding at times. Please don't tell them to just suck it up… research their specific brand of depression and work with them, help them.

I have been putting off this issue for a while. No Autist (Autistic Spectrum Individual) wants to discuss meltdowns. Discussing it is a reminder that we are different. If you have an Autist in your life, and you have never experienced a meltdown… You are one of the lucky few.

I have covered tantrum avoidance in this series before, but I do not feel that I have really described what a tantrum is. The following are not terms used by mental health care professionals, but are being used to help express ideas and differentiate certain concepts to make certain things clearer.

Type 1 tantrums:
This is your standard tantrum. Every child is capable of these. A type 1 tantrum is a demonstration of emotion in an attempt to manipulate a situation to their advantage. In this kind of tantrum, the attention of someone else is REQUIRED. There will be glances to make sure that they are being observed. Traditionally, this is the type of tantrum that can be made to go away by ignoring it.

Type 2 tantrums:
If you have children – Autistic or otherwise, you have seen this kind of tantrum before. It often leads to long, heart breaking crying jags and doesn't seem to respond to normal tantrum coping mechanisms.
Ignoring a type 2 tantrum will not solve or diffuse the issue.

Type 2 tantrums are the difficult ones to deal with. These are an outburst of emotion due to excessive stimulation – whether it be sensory stimulation or something far more insidious – emotional stimulation. All Autists, regardless of age, are capable of this kind of tantrum. These tantrums are rarely used to achieve any specific goal. Well, that is not entirely accurate.

There will be a goal to this type of tantrum. To remove the offending stimuli.

The term, emotional stimulation, can be confusing. It can be anything from an unfulfilled desire (for an object, food, a different stimulus, being alone, or a change of environment). It can come from unwanted attention, a desire for attention, an argument, disagreement or difference of opinion.

Tantrum vs Meltdown:
I have heard parents say that they don't think that there is any difference between a tantrum and a meltdown. They say that a meltdown is just a bigger type two tantrum. To a certain extent, this is true… but I do not feel that it is wholly accurate.

A meltdown MAY share the same mechanisms as a tantrum at the start of the event. However, once it shifts from tantrum to meltdown, it changes. The following information is presented as someone who has had meltdowns in his adult life.

Yes, as an adult, I have had tantrums. Sometimes the manic cycles of comorbid bi-polar or sensury issues of autism lead to a build up of pressure, emotionally speaking. The outbursts from this emotional pressure can be intense, sometimes long lasting and horrific. The main thing about these events is that (in spite of the irritation, anger and irrationality) we are rarely tempted to be violent. There may be flailing as a reaction to continued stimulation, but this is not intended to be violent.

The mechanisms of a tantrum are actually a defense mechanism of the Autist brain to remove offending stimulus and attempt to regain an emotional equilibrium.

In a meltdown… this changes… If the mechanisms are the same, then I can only say that they are in overdrive… on steroids… Often a tantrum will be in response to stimuli, either physical, sensory or emotional… Once we pass from tantrum, into meltdown, those mechanisms are magnified to the point that they stop being a defense mechanism and instead, shift from a coping device into actually being the problem. They feedback on themselves and cause a dissonant event.

Symptoms of a meltdown are as follows:
- During a meltdown, the Autist does not care if they are being observed, they are absorbed in their own issues.
- They will not consider there own safety and stand risk of causing themselves or others harm.
- A meltdown is a bit like a hurricane. Once it starts, it will continue under its own power. The only thing to do is ride it out.
- While a tantrum seems out of control, it is not. In a meltdown, no one (not NT helper, parent or Autist) feels like they are in control… and they are not.
- The causes of a meltdown may be caused by an unmet need or an inability to adapt to an environmental change… but once it reaches the meltdown stage, nothing will be able to satisfy them until the event passes.

The tactics used to diffuse a tantrum will not be effective once it crosses over into a meltdown. This means that, aside from severity, the one thing that sets a tantrum apart from meltdown is the inability to diffuse it.

When you are faced with the a meltdown situation, and it becomes clear that the event cannot be avoided, it is best to accept that and try your best to not add stimuli to the situation. it will only serve to make the event worse. As hard as it may be for you to do this, it is best to simply endure. Accept that this is a force of nature that you are facing down.

At the end of the meltdown, after care is very very important.

You AND your Autist are going to be exhausted by what has happened. Your Autist may be physically battered and bruised. They will most certainly be emotionally battered. They will need comfort, love and support.

This next statement may upset some Autists or their care-takers, pet NTs or parents, but it is my personal opinion. I believe that the aftermath of a meltdown is harder on higher functioning Autists… I have spoken to the parent's of low functioning Autists and to some lower functioning Autists themselves, and the meltdown seem to be forgotten by the Autist after a relatively short amount of time. For those of us who are higher functioning, we are stuck with the memory and realization that we behaved in a way that runs completely counter to the way we normally behave and feel. We were mean, rude, vulgar and possibly violent to those we love… we may have broken favorite objects, furniture, tools or even ourselves…

And we are stuck with it. It is seared into our brains, permanently. Some of us are stuck with the memory of what said and did… and it leads to guilt. I can tell you, from personal experience, that it sucks. So, after a meltdown, be sure to provide the much needed after care. Give your Autist the love, caring and possibly space they need to process what has just happened.

28 – Things that Every Autist Wishes You Knew

Since this guide is designed to facilitate communication and interpersonal relationships between Neurotypicals and Aspies, this entry is long over due. This is a list I have compiled from all over the web of things that Autistic Spectrum Individuals wish that Neurotypicals knew. These are not in any particular order, so please do not lend weight to them by the order presented.

- Often, we tell people we cannot do something. There is a HUGE difference between I can't and I won't. Often NTs can't wrap their minds around this. If we tell you that we can't do something… it is not a refusal to do it. There is a very real possibility that we are actually unable to do what has been asked of us, either because of dissonance, sensory issues, or a lack of clarity in instruction.

- Due to the nature of Autism, many of us are afflicted with sensory issues. Things that you take for granted… sights, smells, tastes, tactile sensations and sounds that you take for granted and often don't even notice… are sometimes overwhelming… Sometimes, they can even be downright painful.

- We are visually oriented. Telling us how to do something will probably just frustrate you. SHOW US how to do something. You will be pleased with the results.

- There is no autistic appearance. Autists come in all shapes and sizes. Anyone who tells you differently is wrong.

- Don't touch unless you are invited to do so. Touch is an

incredibly intimate experience. If we don't know you to the point where we are totally comfortable with you, we won't welcome a touch event. If you are told that you can touch, hug, etc… take it as the compliment it is.

- We are not defined by our condition. This is often explained by the saying "I am not autistic. I have autism." I dislike the wording of this… as this is a bit like, "I am not autistic… I am autistic." I do, however agree with the sentiment… We have autism… one NT might have chronic halitosis, another might be short or bald… These possibly prejudicial conditions do not define the NT. Why should being an Autist (Autistic Spectrum Individual) define us?

- We are terribly literal. Colorful language can be difficult. Hyperbole can be extremely confusing… When you exaggerate, we try to picture what you just said. Idioms, emotional connotations to words, sarcasm, metaphor, simile and many other linguistic constructs will be lost on your Autist as they rely on creative use of words that we have problems with. We will often be confused when the meanings used or implied do not mesh with the dictionary definitions of words.

- We will remember a wide range of trivial and useless information. If we are babbling about something, imparting information this means two things a) you have found a topic we are interested in and b) we trust you and value your opinion enough to share what we know. Cherish this… it is rare.

- Social interactions are difficult for us. We WANT to be part of them… sometimes… if you see us trying… HELP US… explain nuances, help us tell the other people in the situation that we are autistic and you are our NT to Autist Translator…

- Eye contact is difficult for us. We're not sure why, but it is true. My personal belief is that this is a left over instinct… an atavism, if you will. In nature, eye contact is a form of challenge, a contest for dominance. For most of us, the residual conflict that is inherent to this challenge can be problematic. It can lead to dissonance, emotional discomfort and even pain.

- Tantrums will happen. Please try to understand. We are not ill behaved… It is a stress response. We are attempting to remove an anxiety causing stimulus. It is not something we can control. On the same note, meltdowns can and will happen. Just remember that these are as hard, if not harder on us than they are on you.

- Our cognitive processes are logical and literal. Our emotional processes are not. This causes internal conflict and stress… Which leads to over stimulation… when we catch feelings, it can be very difficult for us to deal with.

- Since our sense processes are somewhat scrambled, we perceive words differently. Some words will have sensations attached to them. They can be slimy, fuzzy, prickly, sour… and we will avoid those words to the point of bad reactions to them.

- We will have obsessions. We cannot help it. Our brain is just like this.

- Due to the way our brain works, when things do not line up with our cognitive model of the world… it does not seem that we are the one who is weird. We won't think that until someone points it out to us. while it sounds egocentric, we are wired in such a way that it seems as the world is filled with odd, irrational, loud, emotionally unstable and rude people… We are not truly delusional… the behavior of others is completely foreign to our cognitive functioning.

- When we have feelings they are bigger. Our emotions are extremely potent. While emotion over coming rationality is rare… it can be horrifying… when we get angry, we are enraged… when we are sad, we are devastated… when we are glad, we are MORE than happy… when we love… we do it with EVERY quanta of our being.

29 – Aspies, Bullies and Being Bullied

This is a hot button topic for parents and Autists (Autistic Spectrum Individuals) alike. Before I get into the meat of this story, I want to provide a little background on this topic as it applies to me.

As you have probably surmised from this series, I am an Autism Self Advocate. I am writing this series in an attempt to facilitate Autist/NT communication. I do this for a variety of reasons… some of which are selfish; I am tired of the misinformation surrounding my condition. Some of my reasons are not – I hate to see the suffering that is inflicted on Autists that could easily be avoided by an increased understanding of the Autistic condition.

To that end, I will attempt to facilitate communication between Autists and Neurotypicals and in some situations, between Autists and other Autists.

One of the biggest problems that I encounter is that, often, there is a disconnect between language and meaning. The English language is, by its nature, terribly imprecise. When communicating with NTs, Autists will often find that their grasp of language and the definitions of words is rarely as good as they thing. When communicating with Autists, few (even the Autist in question) realize that language use stimulates the sensory centers of the brain. Since Autists, as a rule, tend to have sensory issues… This can lead to problems. Certain words have a feel, a color and a taste. As such, communication can be an overwhelming experience. What's worse, with the miswiring associated with sensory issues, language can be problematic and difficult.

In my attempts to help, I have stuck to my guns with one concept – "The burden of communication lies with the communicator." This is a truism with me and, to a bigger extent, with the world. If you want to communicate, it is your responsibility to make yourself understood. If you are constantly misunderstood, then perhaps, just perhaps, the issue is with your communication, not with those around you.

I have attempted to help several people who had problems making themselves understood. Some have been thankful – others have told me that I, and everyone around them are just too stupid to understand their words. In one such situation, when the "genius" was screaming (metaphorically speaking – it was on a forum) at me because of my lack of intelligence, I explained that I was attempting to help. Another member of the board jumped in defending the "genius".

After one or two posts, the "defender" called me a bully and started harassing me. The "defender" refused to accept my statement that I was (HONESTLY) trying to help. (Even the Moderators saw that this was the case) The harassment continued to the point that he was bullying me. I received private messages stating that other members saw that I was trying to help and that this individual had taken anti-bullying to the farthest extreme and become a bully himself.

I was appalled, angry and outraged… It was really a disheartening experience to be called a bully when I LITERALLY just want to help.

That being said… bullying is a big problem for Autists… we are different, and as members of a species of primates, that means we incite a violent streak in the other primates on an instinctive level. It is so deeply ingrained into the primate psyche and physiology, that they often don't realize that they are doing it.

Before I continue, I want to put a couple things in

perspective… Studies on the topic of bulling have found that 54-71% of children (depending on source) feel that they have been bullied. One study focused on students that were considered "popular" and found that the percentages held true for them as well. So… A majority of children feel as if they have been bullied.

As I have discussed previously, a failure to communicate properly can and often does, lead to cognitive dissonance. As does the concept that we have misinterpreted social situations. Now add to that, a hostility that makes no sense to us. Most times, bullying is a response to something that was witnessed at an earlier point in time. So, from the Autists standpoint, we are typically just being… doing our own thing… literally, minding our own business (as it is often difficult to do anything else)… When unnecessary hostility, violence, or just general mean-ness is leveled without apparent rhyme or reason – the consequences, psychologically speaking can be devastating.

The Mardi Gras horror story of Emily Meuller is a prime example of this. When ONE MAN (A**H*LE is more like it), made a comment that is worthy of being referred to as bullying – Emily just wanted to go home. It ruined her favorite time of year. One comment… I have not spoken to her, but I can only assume from my own experiences that this was a terribly dissonant event. Now… Imagine the constant verbal, mental and sometimes physical abuse that is visited upon children who are bullied. (For the record, there was a happy ending to the Emily story… it was called Emily Gras.)

Now, let's take a step back from childhood bullying and its effects… The event I described with the "genius" and the "defender"… that was recently… I am 38 years old. And I was a victim of online bullying. It happens. It happens more often than you would expect. Adults think that they are better than they were as children. The only difference is that they have a bigger vocabulary and refrain (sometimes) from physical violence… but the meanest things that have ever been said to me were by other adults.

So the question becomes – how can we avoid bullying.

For the younger Autists (children, teens, and young adults), the best solution is to start socialization as early in their lives as possible. If we are taught what certain social cues mean and how to interact with other children – it is possible to be a little odd, as opposed to straight out weird. Further, teaching them that they need to find the RIGHT friends. They need to know that the right people will appreciate them for who and what they are.

For adult Autists, this can be a little harder. Because we live in a politically correct world that obsessed with "correct" speech, we have been inundated with the concept that there is nothing wrong with us. That we are just different. While this is all well and good and boosts self image and confidence… I have to ask you… If this is a true statement… why are you here? Why are you reading my blog? If there is nothing wrong with us, why do I need to make a guide to NT/Aspie relations and communication? The first thing that is required is for the Autist to come to the realization that there is indeed something different, wrong or not normal about us. Once that happens, you can move forward with many of the same lessons that are required for younger Autists…

What does this all have to do with bullying? Honestly, it is a technique to avoid it – blending with, or at least communicating with NTs is the the most effective way to deal with the topic.

What happens when it can't be avoided? The hardest lesson for us to learn is to WALK AWAY… While there IS something wrong with us, the voices of the IGNORANT should mean nothing to us. This is incredibly difficult to do, but must be done. After we walk away… it comes down to after care. We will need assurances that it is not us… that these people are idiots who do not have the cognitive ability to understand and grasp that they are really only hurting themselves…

It is hard… VERY hard for the Autist, and those who love them… but understanding can prevent, solve and ameliorate the situation… Not understanding from those who would bully us, but yours and your Aspie's.

30 – A Schism of Reasoning – Why We NEED the Classification of Disease.

This part of the series is a meandering essay on the negative perceptions associated with certain words, my thoughts on perceptions of language, NT perceptions and a framework of understanding needed for advocacy. Some of the conversations I was in while researching this specific issue were a bit heated… and I will admit, I got angry… if I offended anyone… I am sorry.

Let me start by saying that this essay may alienate many of my readers. It is not my intent to do so. While this essay is directed at the Autists who read, it is also intended to be an eye opener for those NTs who care about us. Especially parents… the attitudes I find damaging to the greater good of Autists everywhere start at childhood.

Back when I started this series, I made a post that stated Autism is a Disease. I'm not going to rehash the information and views expressed there, as there is little point in repetition for repetition's sake. I am however, going to comment on the need for acknowledgment of this status.

Recently, I have been in several conversations where fellow Autists have vehemently denied and decried the label of "disease" for Autistic Spectrum Disorders. I will admit… It all boils down to negative associations that this specific word carries.

The source of my frustration is that when confronted with the medical definition of the word, many will focus on one or two Aspects of the definition.

For a refresher, here is the medical definition of disease:
"an impairment of the normal state of the living animal or

plant body or one of its parts that interrupts or modifies the performance of the vital functions, is typically manifested by distinguishing signs and symptoms, and is a response to environmental factors (as malnutrition, industrial hazards, or climate), to specific infective agents (as worms, bacteria, or viruses), to inherent defects of the organism (as genetic anomalies), or to combinations of these factors"

I, for one, don't see the negative connotations of this definition, so I asked. I asked Autists on several message boards and forums… I asked them, "Just what and why is there a stigma associated with this word?"

The responses fell into one of several generalized categories.

1. The definition that you have provided is so vague that it can include, almost literally, anything.
2. No one has ever died of Autism.
3. Autism is not caused by a germ.
4. Impairment… I don't have an impairment…I am just wired differently.

These responses, while still baffling to me, did provide a little bit of insight into what we are facing…

Let's take a look at the first argument…

Disease is such a vague term… anything that is abnormal can be classified as a disease.
That is kind of the point. Disease is a vague term… because it describes anything, literally, anything that is wrong with the body. This has been a source of frustration for me… A major source, honestly… Until I realized that Autists and Aspies like things cut and dried. We don't like vagueness in our lives, and a term that is as broad as this one is, can be a major source of frustration.

I am not here to try to convince anyone to use the term… but that is the wonderful thing about language… no matter your personal opinion, if the definition fits, then the word applies… whether or not we like the vagueness of it, it its… but let's look at it another way… as opposed to being a vague word… it is relatively precise when you look at it from a different standpoint… If the answer to, "Are all your biological systems (body and mind) functioning within the established mean and norms for a human of your age, sex and gender?" – is no… then the word disease applies.

The second argument actually made me laugh.
"No one has ever died of Autism."
I actually laughed so hard that I had an asthma attack… And I would like to apologize to the several people that made that statement. I know you did not realize that I had done that, but I wronged you on my end, I am sorry.

There is an inherent problem with this argument… Not all diseases are fatal – especially the genetic ones. Lupus, pophyria, rheumatoid arthritis, Hutchinson-Guilford progeria, Graves' disease… These are all drastically life altering, but not fatal unto themselves.

"Autism is not caused by a germ."
This is the reason that I listed genetic disorders… none of these are caused by germs, parasites or pathogens… As such, it is evident that diseases do not have to be caused by any of these things. Further… I came to the realization that this argument is actually firmly rooted in one of the diagnostic criteria for Autism… A fascination or preoccupation with parts or pieces of something. Our very condition makes us lock onto that ONE part of the definition, in spite of the fact that it says, "This, This OR This."

That being said, one must also remember that the causes of Autistic Spectrum Disorders are unknown at this time… It may very well be caused by a germ… either in us, or genetic damage dealt to one or both of our parents… we just don't know.

"I am just wired differently."
This is the one that has been a major sticking point for me. I believe that this statement has it's roots in the recent movement in self esteem. The "we're all okay," movement as I have called it. And this is great… The fact that many Autists, high and low functioning alike can demonstrate this level of self esteem does my heart a great amount of good.

These are all valid emotional arguments and I (after getting angry and annoyed beyond belief at perceived ignorance) actually revel in the diversity of views presented… but this stance, on the whole, hurts the Autistic Spectrum community.

When discussing the state of care for Autists, there are several things that crop up over and over and over… There is a perceived need for:
- **Autism Advocacy** – someone who understand that can tell the world about us and be our voice.
- **Treatment** – coping skills, education, training and medication if needed
- **Autism Awareness and Education** – a need to educate the public about Autistic Spectrum Disorders.
- **Services for Autists** – this is a catch all, assistance, assistants, access to the three points above, and the like

So, let's look at these desired steps from the standpoint of an NT. I have been assured that while the following statements are offensive to the Autists who read them… your average NT would at least think these things.

Advocacy:

You don't have a disease… you are just wired differently…
Why do you need advocacy then? If there is nothing wrong with
you, what is there to advocate? You come from all walks of life,
every race, all the genders, both sexes, different countries… The
only thing that you have in common is Autism… So… what is
there that needs to be advocated?

Treatment:
Isn't treatment for sick people? Why do you need to learn
social skills? Just get out there and talk to people. Pfft!
Medicine? For what… you being a social reject? Do they make
a pill for geek? What? Why are you mad at me? You're the one
that said you are just different… So's that band geek, or that
goth… Right… overstimulated, what ever… You're just
looking for attention.

Awareness and Education:
Look, I am tolerant of your behavior, but I don't have to like
it. Why do I have to be aware of you… especially if there is
nothing wrong with you. So, you're wired differently… every
person is unique, suck it up and deal with it…like the rest of us.

Services for Autists:
There's nothing wrong with you… You said so, yourself.
Why do you need special services?

What it boils down to is that we can't have it both ways.
Autists are people with special needs, whether it be alone time,
understanding, a helper, or more… But the stance that many
take, "There is nothing wrong with me – I'm just wired
differently," hurts us as a whole.

While groups like Autism Speaks do damage to the reputation
of Autists in the eyes of the public, we do more damage to
ourselves with this stance. The concept that there is nothing
wrong with us automatically conjures an expectation of

behavior in the minds of the NTs around us. By demonstrating the behaviors associated with Autistic Spectrum disorders in the presence of NTs after making this claim, we set ourselves up for ridicule and worse.

The NTs of the world are not bad people, but their culture and brains are wired so that odd behavior and such requires a specific response – ridicule. Autists that are ridiculed are often offended by the ridicule and they are right to be… BUT… by insisting that there is nothing wrong with us, we are giving up any claim we have to be able to stop the ridicule, comments, stares or worse – bullying.

By insisting that we are just different, we are stating that we don't need treatment, advocacy, or special education or even awareness of our condition, because we are just like everyone else. This series, would be unnecessary and, frankly, arrogant if there wasn't something wrong with us.

We demand concessions of behavior, yearn for awareness and understanding of the NTs around us… But if there is nothing wrong with us, why are these things needed? That's right… if there is nothing wrong with us, we don't need any of these things. Period.

Yet, herein lies the paradox, we do need these things. We crave and desire the companionship that (honestly) only NTs can provide… but these NTs have to make adjustment to their modes of thought, speech, awareness and feelings to deal with us… If we do not have special needs; if we are normal; if there is nothing wrong with us; this is supreme arrogance.

Think about it. If another Autist was in your group of friends and his special interest was trains (I know, but it was the first word that popped into my mind), and would not stop talking about it… ever… and you never got a chance to talk about your special interest… at all… ever, you would be upset by this. This person, in spite of their Autism, would be considered self centered… I know, because I've seen it happen…

So, think about this… NTs don't have special interests… When you gabble on about your interest and they listen politely, and in some few cases have enough information to discuss with you… They have made a concession in their behavior based on your Autism. They understand, because they know that there is something wrong with you and are more than willing to accept it and deal with it because they did research, and cherish your friendship.

Without that, from an NT standpoint – you are just an obsessed fanboy with no concern for other people's interests, time, thoughts or opinions.

So, you have to ask yourself this – In spite of the feeling that you like yourself and feel that there is nothing wrong with you, do you want to be viewed as an arrogant ass with no empathy or ability/willingness to connect with others? Because if we drop the Autistic Spectrum Disorder… that's what most NTs see us as… and if we don't have a disease, if nothing is wrong with us, then there is no need for that diagnosis.

Simply put – without there being an underlying cause, there is no point in even considering yourself Autistic. Use the word you want – syndrome, disorder, disease… they, literally, mean the same thing… But if there is nothing wrong with you, then the diagnostic criteria are nothing more than an odd, misplaced Astrology sign that is entirely too accurate.

And here is the point where the tough love comes in. If you feel there is nothing wrong with you, then why are you even claiming to be an Autist? If there is nothing wrong with you, then why are you taking the time to bother telling people, research your condition? Why are you telling people that you are an Autist, and then telling them that there is nothing wrong with you? That kind of double talk is confusing to NTs and Autists alike and is damaging to us as a whole… The NTs you tell this eventually come to the conclusion that Autism is either a made up diagnosis, or is being used as an excuse.

What's worse, though, is that this attitude gets back to lawmakers, who are notoriously lacking in intelligence and they believe it. They decide where the money for special services goes… and if Autism and Asperger's are made up… if there's nothing wrong with these people, why should we give money to services that will help these fakers? You are in a situation where your self esteem is hurting people who need these services… Your self esteem is directly effecting me.

And lastly, if there is nothing wrong with you… you literally have NO RIGHT to ask for understanding or accommodation in any situation as it pertains to your Autism. Think about it. This isn't just my interpretation, but this is how NTs feel about it. They will make concessions for friends, but as an Autist, we often need accommodation for people who don't even know us… it happens… and you are asking them for preferential treatment without any reason at all… After all, there is nothing wrong with you.

I know this essay has rubbed a lot of people the wrong way, but I hope that it has also inspired thought. In the modern world, we need to be self advocates, educators of those around us, and take our treatment plans into our own hands… but we can't do that if we are in denial. I see it as a two edged sword, self esteem is a wonderful thing and lets people survive what seems insurmountable obstacles… but if it gets in the way of being realistic, we lose all that we have worked for and are working towards.

For the record… I felt the same way… but as I started the self assessment and analysis that led to this series and my understanding of the mechanisms behind my condition, I had to face the fact that there is, indeed something wrong with me. It was difficult to accept and even harder to adjust to… but it has not diminished my self worth in any way… it has given me the freedom to explore exactly what is going on in my brain and help others understand it… If we live in denial, we really have no way of moving forward, or even understanding who we are.

31 – ADHD and Autistic Spectrum Disorders

I have talked about comorbid conditions a bit in this series, and as I find the time, ability and focus, I am going more in depth into some of specific conditions. ADHD is one of them. ADHD, is one that I suffer from.

I have been striving to explain ADHD (Attention deficit hyperactivity disorder) to those who don't suffer from it. I use the word suffer – but, personally, I enjoy it. It allows me to get a lot done… Well… in short bursts.

I have explained it before… "Ask me about my attention deficit disorder… or pie… or my cat. Wait! A dog!. I have a bike. Do you like TV? I saw a rock. Hi." This really doesn't explain it… it doesn't even begin to touch on it – but tonight, I found the perfect way to explain it.

Moulin Rouge.

I know you heard me, but I'll say it again – just to be sure.

Moulin Rouge is exactly like what it is like to have severe ADHD. If you don't know what I mean. Watch the following video (https://youtu.be/qpVFnNNi9lE) Pay especially close attention to the disjointed nature of the editing. Pay close attention to the fact there there are about 400 different ideas all clashing together in this 6 minutes of video. The images whirl around in a mish-mash of… glorious chaos.

Now, take a moment to reflect on what you just saw. Take each of these warring images off the screen – take each of them and make it a thought. That is what ADHD is like.

I mean seriously… something that was described as "One of the most amazing cinematic love stories ever committed to celluloid" makes me feel like the movie was laying in wait and ambushed me… The love story starts in an elephant's butt! (I can't make this shit up)

I mean let's take a look at this from an existential standpoint. Ironically enough, I believe that all love stories firmly belong in an elephant's butt… and the fact that this elephant's butt had a heart shaped locket over it's sphincter is an accurate expression of this symbolism.

Look at some of the characters… there is a dwarf (Toulouse-Lautrec), a narcoleptic Armenian, a kid whose name translates to Brat Cheese, Nini Legs-in-the-Air and a potions master from Hogwarts. I think there is a real correlation between this character list and real life.

Next…

What? You want me to explain that? I'm already on to the next point!

I don't have to explain myself to you… I mean, really… this is an essay on ADHD and it would really drive the point home if I just… moved on.

Very well…

Brat Cheese… There are a bunch of small things in the world that are a pain in the ass… even if you don't sweat it, they are still there… Brats… and… ummm… they smell like cheese? NO! I got it… Cheese! It's a metaphor… cheese means farts… flatulence… we all have to deal with the bratty, stinky little things that ruin our life… "Don't sweat the small stuff!" and it's ALL small stuff.

Nini Legs-in-the-Air… hmmm… well… It's a statement that

we're supposed to enjoy those very things that make us human… Those instinctual things that we make us human… appreciation of beauty, the need to create and every once in a while, the need to … well… Have the sex. It's kind of like those things in life that feel sooo good… sex, smiles, laughing, a warm rain, sunsets, kittens… Weird emo pop songs…

The narcoleptic Armenian… I can do this one… Ummm… narcoleptic Armenian… narcoleptic Armenian… Got it! There is a need of the body to do some things. Like the aforementioned sex, eat salty foods, have a steak… and the human need for naps. The Armenian represents the need to just GIVE IN to your baser desires sometimes…By ignoring those baser, instinctual needs… we are diluting that which makes us strong!

Ok… Toulouse-Lautrec… a bohemian… midget? Little Person? Dwarf? Bohemian: a person, as an artist or writer, who lives and acts free of regard for conventional rules and practices. AHA!!! Toulouse-Lautrec represents the need of modern man to step away from conventional world and take a break, enjoying something that we don't normally… like a tulip, a star-scape, dancing, kittehs (Cats are weird – damn you!), cartoons…

There! I did it… The whole damn movie is metaphor for life-lessons that we must learn…

I don't like it. I don't like it at all… I feel like it bludgeoned my senses and committed sexual harassment (i.e. fucked) some pop culture…

ANYWAY…

Oh? You say I forgot one? The potions master from Hogwarts? I could of sworn I covered him. OH OH OH! I saw a rock, once… Hi.

Now… How does this relate to Autistic Spectrum Disorders? Well… let's look at it logically… We Autists have problems with concentration already… When ADHD kicks in, these problems are exacerbated. We cannot focus at all, and even hyperfocus is ceases to work. Your Aspie may end up frustrated, angry, or worse – having a tantrum or a melt-down.

From a personal standpoint – ADD/ADHD can be horrific… I will sit down and try to edit a video, write, watch a movie or even play a video game… All things that are my special interests… all things that should allow me to focus with a supreme will… and there are times… when I can't… I just can't. I will sit at the computer staring for hours… something that should take a couple of hours doesn't happen… my brain won't let me…

So, in the grand scheme of things, if your Aspie lives with ADD or ADHD, be prepared for some additional emotional trauma… They may not mean to be upset… but having intense desire to do something but being prevented from doing it by your very brain is extremely upsetting. As with everything else dealing with our condition, we have to have a little understanding… if your Aspie is diagnosed with ADD/ADHD along an Autism Spectrum Disorder – when there is a bout of unspecified and undefined frustration, ask them if they are having problems concentrating. Chances are, they will be immensely grateful for this LITTLE demonstration of understanding.

32 – Sometimes, I just don't have anything to say!

As an Autist, I find myself in an odd position when dealing with NTs who do not know me, or my condition. NTs spend a lot of time talking. I mean a lot of time. Constantly. If you don't believe me, take a couple minutes the next time you are out and about and listen. No… Seriously… do it… Listen carefully… I believe you will find that the conversations around you that you are bathed in have little, if any, substance.

Inconsequentials have little place in conversation for an Autist. It falls under the heading of "Small Talk" and we really don't do it. More importantly, I don't think we CAN do it. NTs will discuss the weather… at length… they will talk about how hot it was last year at this time and how we need rain, we've been in a drought and how the weather is different now than it was when they were young.

When you ask an Autist about the weather… you will get a response that pertains to the here and now. "It's hot." – "It's raining." There is nothing more, there is nothing less… because the weather, unless it is a Special Interest for your Autist, the weather (or any other small talk subject, for that matter) will not elicit any substantial response.

As a student of human nature, I can see the point in many forms of small talk. By talking about inconsequentials, both parties are able to ascertain certain attitudes, assess conversational (and to a certain extent, intellectual and emotional) compatibility, and read micro-expressions in a controlled situation. Further, NTs use these situations and interactions to establish a pecking order, status and social dominance.

Most of these things are lost on the Autist. We are unable to read micro-expressions. Compatibility for us (emotional, intellectual and conversational) is a more direct thing for us than it is for NTs. We don't need to do a verbal dance to ascertain it. Dominance and social standing is meaningless…

So, as you can see, small talk is a relatively fruitless thing for Autists…

The problem, as I see it, is that we are all primates. Primates use constant communication as a matter of safety. Primates, in the wild, will constantly chatter at one another… This is so that the entire troupe (that is what a group of monkeys or apes is called) can keep track of each other. If the vocal stresses of a member of the troupe change, the rest of the members know there is reason for caution. If a voice stops… the troupe knows that there is something severely wrong.

So, you see, there is a reason for it all… Autists are either more in touch with our instincts are able to ascertain the danger of our situation or (and this is more likely) we just don't have those instincts. As such, the constant noise required by NTs for proper social interaction and comfort is uncomfortable for Autists.

Since we don't have these instincts, we come across as odd in conversation. If we are on a topic that is one of our Special Interests, we cannot shut up about it. We will talk and talk and talk… and talk… and talk… If it is something we don't have interest, or knowledge in, we are quiet – to the point of silence. There are a couple reasons for that. The first being that we all have a history of personal embarrassment from sounding like an idiot, so we don't talk when we don't know anything about the topic. Secondly, silence allows us to learn. When we are surrounded by people who are knowledgeable on the topic being discussed, we can learn all of the information that they present in the conversation. Knowledge… is addicting…

The crux of the matter is that if you don't talk… just the right amount, you are screwed when dealing with NTs. If they happen to touch on your Special Interests, and we do what we do… Then you are arrogant and can't be bothered to worry about what other people say. If you are quiet, and listening… you are arrogant and the conversation (or people IN the conversation) are beneath us and we are showing contempt for them by not contributing.

I wish I had a guide for when it was acceptable to speak, when it was acceptable to be quiet, when either was required… but I don't know. I really don't. Even after all of my experience with people watching… I just don't know.

So, I offer this advice to NTs who have a pet Aspie or Autist… If you are in a conversation and your Autist is there… Find a way to include them… introduce them and explain to everyone that they are an Autist. Believe it or not, this will help the NTs in the conversation accept that your Autistic Spectrum Individual will not be judged because they are too talky or too quiet…

If you have an Aspie in your life, then you have invariably encountered the issue of money… Since we tend towards obsessive behaviors with Obsessive Compulsive Disorder and the obsessive nature of Special Interests, money has always and will always be an issue for your Aspie.

Studies show that between 53% and 68% of Autists (Autistic Spectrum Individuals) are unemployed. Of those, roughly half are considered disabled – i.e. unemployable. As such, we have little in the way of income at most times. Though, honestly, even if your Aspie is a productive member of society, they will still have these problems… unless they are extremely successful.

The reason for this is that, without the proper survival skill training, your Aspie is not equipped to survive in the modern world. They will be driven to spend their money on Obsessive pursuits and Special Interests.

The root of this is the the way your Aspie's decision making processes work.

Simply put, NTs have a spectrum of likes and dislikes. Their decision making process is based on a subconscious comparison of likes, dislikes, desires and aversions from moment to moment. Since their likes and dislikes lie on a spectrum, this decision making process is relatively easy.

In your Aspie, this is not the case… Autists don't have have this spectrum of thought, as a general rule. We tend to see things in absolutes… It's black or white… or we don't have an a opinion. Without the spectrum of desire, it is often difficult for Autists to make decisions. Sometimes, the dissonance of warring desires or aversions can cause an Autist to have issues, sometimes resulting in a mental vapor-lock.

This inability to make a decision at times can be a real problem for an Autist. Anxiety, stress, and the symptomology that accompany them can result. After a lifetime of this anxiety, Autists can and do avoid any situation where they will be forced to make a decision of this nature.

These problems result from our likes and dislikes being rated at a 10 or -10 on the spectrum of desire, respectively. So, when confronted with the focus of OCD or one of our Special Interests… we are relieved. You see, OCD and Special Interests are different from other subjects. They don't obey the standard 10/-10 rule. OCD focuses and Special Interests fall into a +1 category. So, any decision that involves one of these things becomes an easy decision…

Allow me to explain… We use the same mechanism as NTs to make our decisions, but we often counter issues with our all or nothing intellectual processes. When we have an option of a 10 vs. an 11, the decision is an easy one to make… even if it is the WRONG choice to make. Even if we KNOW that the decision will cause problems or complications later on, we will still make it, as it is one we can do without hesitation.

If we have a choice between saving some money and buying something for one of our many collections… the 11 wins – collection it is! If we have to eat well or get something for one of our Special Interests… the 11 wins – and we'll eat Ramen Noodles. Or, in my case – SKYLANDERS

It is a fundamental flaw in the data processing mechanism in our brains.

Since we have these issues, we often need help to manage our finances… It may be necessary, especially if your Autist realizes that this is a problem, to help them with this by providing an allowance and keeping control of the rest of the finances. This can be problematic if the Autist doesn't realize that there is an issue. If this is the case, it can be necessary to broach the subject with them.

Now, this isn't to say that ALL Autistic Spectrum Individuals will have money problems… Some of us are lucky enough to have the skills to survive… And I envy these Autists… but the rest of us need some help, don't be afraid to offer it.

34 – Celebrities, Historical Figures and Fictional Characters

This originally started out as a rant. I was furious and I typed up a long diatribe that was supposed to be enlightening and funny and… well I don't know what else it was supposed to be, but what I ended up with was an unintelligible mass of invective gibberish that made little (if any sense) and made me sound like a complete loony.

So… after several weeks, I have decided to re-write it into a more coherent set of thoughts and images and hope that it makes sense to someone.

There is a popular television program on the air called "The Big Bang Theory". One of the characters on this program is Dr. Sheldon Cooper, played by Jim Parsons. There has been a great deal of debate and discussion about this character in the Autism community. The core of the matter has been, "Does Sheldon have Asperger's Syndrome?" The answer seems to be an overwhelming – "YES."

However, I am going to take a contrary stance on this question. I say no. My reasons for this are manifold, but let's start with the fact that the creators of the show state that Sheldon does not have Asperger's Syndrome. But there are other reasons… In one episode, Sheldon's best friend tells him that he is "crazy." Sheldon's response is classic and hilarious – "No. My mother had me tested as a child." Tests of that sort (and I know this from personal experience) are exhaustive and would have resulted in a diagnosis, if the condition were present. I speak from experience.

My sister and I both have exceptionally high I.Q.s. We were both tested in the 180s… due to head trauma, brain damage due to medication, oxygen deprivation when we have died for a short period of time, recreational drug use when younger, and electrical shock over the years, we have both lost quite a few I.Q. points. The thing is, we remember what it was like to be that brilliant. I am not telling you this, but to put things in a bit of perspective.

EXCEPTIONALLY HIGH IQs – ALL OF THEM

According to the show, Sheldon's I.Q. is 187. My sister and I spent a lot of time around people in that range… We have made an observation… At I.Q. 165 and above, there seems to be a fundamental disconnect between the individual and the rest of humanity. For she and I, it was a combination of things – the I.Q. AND the Asperger's Syndrome, but it doesn't negate our observations. As near as I can tell, once a person's I.Q. reaches the 165+ range, several things happen. 1) The amount of knowledge they collect and store dwarfs that of people with normal I.Q.s. 2) They process information at an astounding rate.

The conclusion I have drawn is this: to be able to process this astounding throughput of information, they have to have a slightly different wiring in their brains that allows them to collate data, analyze information and draw conclusions in a way different than those around them. While this may sound like Autistic Perception to you, I believe it is different. Exceptionally high I.Q. people do not have a fundamental disconnect on social cues and the finer points of of human interaction… They are, however, most often distracted by thinking. They think big, fast and intricate thoughts… They do this at all times – while driving, sleeping, eating, and while talking to you.

What you have interpreted as the earmarks of an Autistic Spectrum Disorder is actually simple distraction. What they are thinking is so massive in scale that they have precious little mental acuity left to spare on the inconsequential ramblings, repetitions and petty things most people are concerned with. The symptomology is similar, but the mechanisms behind it are different.

That being said, I have a serious question to ask you… Do you REALLY want Dr. Sheldon Cooper as a source of media representation for Autistic Spectrum Disorders? Think about it… do you? Not only is Sheldon Cooper NOT an Autistic Spectrum Individual… He's an ASS! Personally, I want to distance myself from his diagnosis as much as possible.

Individuals with Asperger's Syndrome tend to have a higher I.Q. than representative groups, on average. This fact, however, is misleading. You see, to be diagnosed with Asperger's syndrome, there can be no sign of mental retardation. If mental retardation is present, then the individual, by default, is diagnosed with Autism. So, when calculating the I.Q.s. of Autists, Aspies have removed the lower I.Q. scores from our pool, skewing our numbers.

Because of this, Aspies tend to think that we are, on the whole, smarter than everyone around us… Unfortunately, this is patently untrue.

Because of our odd thought patterns and the weirdness that are required for genius level thinking, Aspies assume, often wrongly, that anyone with a spark of madness and genius is one of us…

I have seen attempts to claim Einstein, Shakespeare, Newton and more.

Stop it. No… really… stop doing that… I mean it…

There are a large number of people who were brilliant in their fields that have been diagnosed with Asperger's Syndrome…

One of the most notable is Hans Asperger… but the following is a partial list – Isaac Asimov, John Denver, Glenn Gould, Jim Henson, Alfred Hitchcock, Howard Hughes, Andy Kaufman, L. S. Lowry, Charles Schulz, Andy Warhol, Tony Benn, Pip Brown "Ladyhawke", Charles Dickinson, Bob Dylan, Joseph Erber, Bill Gates, Crispin Glover, Al Gore, Jeff Greenfield, David Helfgott, Garrison Keillor, Paul Kostabi, Kevin Mitnick, John Motson, John Nash, Keith Olbermann, Michael Palin, Oliver Sacks, James Taylor, Robin Williams, Jamie Hyneman, Seth Engstrom…

We can't go back in time and talk to people that have already died… and so we can't make a diagnosis. And a diagnosis CANNOT be made by anecdotal evidence… It can't be made without a mental health professional… it requires actual interaction with the person being diagnosed… as such, all of those that are dead and gone, are just that gone… So, who cares if they had Asperger's? We have plenty of brilliant people in our camp. Trying to claim anyone that we feel is a staggering intellect or who is quirky and making a contribution to our lives is arrogant… in the extreme… and when it is not known to be true… it paints us in a bad light in the eyes of the world and those around us.

So… let it go… be happy that humanity is moving forward and stop trying to plant your flag in places where it doesn't belong.

35 – Asperger's is Real

There have been many blog posts dedicated to the ignorant things said to Autistic Spectrum Individuals over the years. Most of these posts are incoherent with rage… With good reason… Many of the things that are said are ignorant, which is not the fault of NTs… they don't know any better… but many of these ignorant things are arrogant, elitist, rude and downright condescending.

However, several of these statements are more problematic than others… They all hinge around a central misconception – that "Asperger's is not a real thing."

Let's start with one of the glaringly obvious issues – over-diagnosis. According to statistics, between 1-110 and 1-88 children in the United States is diagnosed with an Autistic Spectrum Disorder. The media depicts this as an epidemic of Autism. The concept of an epidemic is a bit absurd. Personally, I do not feel that the incidents of Autism have actually increased, but that the diagnoses have become more prevalent as Mental Health Professionals have become more aware of the condition and as pressure from parents has eased.

Yes, I said pressure from parents… and I meant it. I am not a psychiatrist or psychologist, but I have done work in the Mental Health field for a time. I will not go into what my position was as it was essentially menial, but I was privy to sensitive information. One of my best friends was a director of the clinic I worked at.

As such, I witnessed (on more than one occasion) the pressure parents placed on the Mental Health providers. Our current culture has led to a lack of responsibility on the part of parents for their children… I am not condemning parents, but our culture had come around to blame the parents for the actions of their children. This wasn't the case 50 years ago… back then, raising your children correctly was a source of pride… Now, raising them wrong is a source of shame… it is a subtle, but MAJOR difference. As such, parents are DESPERATE to have the cause of their children's issues assigned to anyone but themselves. As a result, they put an amazing amount of pressure on Mental Health Professionals to diagnose a problem.

I have personally witnessed this… in person…

The problem with this is that some Mental Health Professionals feel that there is little harm in an Asperger's diagnosis if it will shut the parents up. After all, what does Asperger's mean, really? It means that the individual is awkward in social situations, has mild obsessive tendencies and is a little weird… right? Right?

You may have an issue with these statements, but I have seen it happen… on more than one occasion.

In many situations, making a diagnosis is more of an art than a science. Part of this is because of the prevalence of mental conditions which leads to Mental Health Professionals only being able to spend very limited time with patients, so diagnosis can be challenging. Diagnosing any mental condition requires that the professional spend time with their patient to observe, and that is just not possible in today's health care climate. Further exacerbating the problem is that different mental problems often have overlapping diagnostic criteria.

That means that it is, in many cases, possible to make a mistake because sometimes there is more than one condition that matches the symptoms as presented. There are additional complications… language is an imprecise tool when attempting to express what one is feeling and experiencing; people find it hard to believe or accept that someone feels differently than they do and will question different perceptions; (I have been told that professionals did not believe that I was capable of what I was thinking, feeling or experiencing.) and medical professionals are often skeptical of people seeking a diagnosis. They encounter people who are trolling for drugs, and the drugs used to treat many medical conditions are psychotropic in nature and as such are valued as recreational pharmaceuticals.

Many nerds and geeks will look at the diagnostic criteria for Asperger's and feel they have it. They have a need to fit in. They crave an Asperger's diagnosis… so that they can do just that. They don't want to just be weird. If there is something wrong with them, then there is a whole new community that they would belong to. And this leads to individuals with a surety of an Autism Spectrum Disorder due to self-diagnosis.

In spite of all this, Autistic Spectrum Disorders and (more specifically) Asperger's Syndrome are very real. Let's put aside the cases of misdiagnosis and self-diagnosed individuals. (There is no such thing as self diagnosis… Period… ONLY a Mental Health Professional can diagnose a mental condition. That is why we can't go to the pharmacy and ask for prescription medications and they require a diagnosis by a trained doctor.) There are a large number of Autistic and Asperger's Syndrome individuals out there.

NT perceptions are skewed in favor of the NT modes of thought. One thing I have noticed about the NT mode of thought is that if something is not visibly wrong, then it is hard for them to grasp that something is ACTUALLY wrong. This leads to statements like "You don't look Autistic!"

All of these things lead NTs to believe that Asperger's is a fake condition. It leads people to believe that anyone who claims to have Asperger's Syndrome is making excuses, is just an asshole or looking for sympathy.

Honestly, that is why I started this series… Autism understanding and awareness can only be achieved through information and education. And that is precisely what I am doing… educating the NTs around us… ALSO… to educate US.

Asperger's Syndrome is a very real thing… And I hope by sharing my experiences and perceptions, I hope that I can make someone's life easier… Yet, I am hoping that some people receive a wake-up call from this series. People who are self-diagnosed need to wake up… If the issues described within do not sound like you at all… then please reconsider. You are harming the Autists around you, and yourself. If these perceptions feel accurate and true for your situation, then please… PLEASE run to a trusted Mental Health Professional and procure a diagnosis. This is the ONLY way you can hope to receive proper treatment.

That being said… If someone you know has Asperger's Syndrome or any other Autistic Spectrum Disorder, you need to accept that… Especially if they have a diagnosis. If they claim to be self-diagnosed, please refer them to the above paragraph… If they refuse, they know deep down that they are not and are afraid of the ridicule associated with that, but do not let your eyes deceive you… Many conditions, especially those affecting mental health are silent, invisible, and will sneak up on you like a ninja.

36 – Workplace Policies and Asperger's

This topic was recently requested on one of the forums I belong to. I have also been asked about it in person on several occasions.

The question is *"Should I tell my boss at work about being an Autistic Spectrum Individual?"*

I am of two minds on this topic. But before I get into that, I want to ask you a question… Would it make your work life any better if they knew?

There are many contributing factors as to whether or not you should advise your workplace about your condition. Do you live in a right to work state? Is your condition contributing to issues in the work place? Are you comfortable doing so? Was your condition known to you when you started working there?

Let's start with the application process. Most companies have a spot on their application that asks something along the lines of, "Do you have any conditions that would prevent you from performing the tasks associated with the position you have applied for?" Many Autists will answer no to this, as we are capable individuals… but later on, we find out that we were wrong – Sensory issues, stress, NT behavior and more make it difficult to complete tasks and work for us. In this case, one has to wonder, should I go ahead and tell the, at this juncture? To this, I can only say, it all depends on the place you are working. If they are decent people, then there is no harm in telling them once it is discovered that you are having issues.

However, many employers are not as accepting and sometimes are downright ignorant, rude or worse in situations like this and will point out that they have it in writing that you do not have any issues that would prevent you from doing your work. They are within their rights to terminate your employment due to a fraudulent application.

So, in this situation, I have to say it is a matter of personal discretion. Most companies will bend over backwards to help a handicapped individual, when they are advised of the condition. Some will not.

If you are comfortable telling your future employer that you have a disability, then do it from the outset. It is much easier to start with everyone knowing than it is to change a paradigm later on in your employment.

"But won't that keep me from getting the job?"

It is a very real possibility that this is the case… but I want you to ask yourself… "Do I want a job where they wouldn't hire me simply because I have an Autistic Spectrum Disorder?" I know the answer to that. I have been through it. The answer, I think, is a resounding, NO. You don't want to work for a company like that.

The reality of it all is that (in the United States, at least) it is illegal for any company to discriminate against anyone in the work place for any disability that they might have. This means that they cannot decide against hiring you based on your disability. Further, they are required, by law, they are required to make reasonable accommodations for disabled individuals in the work place.

What if you are not diagnosed before you start the job and after years of working for a diagnosis, you finally get one? Tell them. Straight up, tell them without hesitation. They cannot terminate your employment for getting sick, and they are required to accommodate (within reason).

I know it can be hard, but we need to be open and honest about our condition. Until recently, I had a lot of problems with admitting my condition… to anyone… One day, I had to take my Big Sister to the hospital… If you have ever been in a hospital emergency room in a big city, then you will understand what I mean when I say that they are rude… in the extreme…

Then the Sister Person said the magic words – "Special Needs Adult." Their attitude changed and suddenly, the people at the hospital were nice, personable, and willing to make concessions to keep her comfortable physically and emotionally. By admitting that she was an Autistic Spectrum Individual, her life became easier.

It took me a while to accept that this is what I needed to do, but I eventually did it. If it weren't for that decision, this series wouldn't exist. Hell, this blog wouldn't exist. Honestly, that is the key to self-advocacy… Acceptance of your condition. If you cannot accept your own differences, limitations and gifts… then you can't expect others to do it.

But I digress… because… well – REASONS!… So it all comes down to the following questions… Do you feel comfortable enough to tell people about your condition? Is your particular brand of Autism such that you need accommodation? Are you having issues with any of your co-workers that would benefit from them knowing about your condition?

If the answer to any of these questions is "yes," then my advice is to tell them. It can't hurt anything.

But the answer is ultimately something that you have to decide for yourself. My sister calls it "The Dollars to Nonsense Equation." Essentially, how much nonsense are you willing to put up with before it becomes an untenable situation? I wish I had a more firm answer for you, but honestly, it needs to be considered on a case by case basis. I, for one, feel that in 99% of cases, the answer to the question is a resounding yes... Tell them.

Knowledge is the first step towards awareness. If they don't know, they can't even begin to become aware... We are each responsible for our own advocacy... Yes, there are groups out there that specialize in Autism Awareness and Advocacy, but not one of them is you. None of them have your particular brand of Autistic Spectrum Disorder... So the best person to talk about your Autistic Experience and Perceptions is you. Don't be afraid to do so.

37 – The Autistic Brain vs. The Neurotypical Brain; Visual Proof

High Definition Fiber Tracking… It's been in the news recently… A LOT.

HDFT is a form of Magnetic Resonance imaging that tacks the diffusion of water through neural tissue that transmits data throughout the brain. The study was conducted in two parts. The first part consisted of scans of of post-mortem human brains. The results were astounding – incredibly detailed maps of the neural tracts in the brain.

The second phase of the study was to take scans of human brains prior to cranial surgery. Using the scans as a guide, the surgeons were able to confirm the accuracy of the project. Then, the same subjects were scanned after surgery were astonishing. Not only did the scans show the neural tracts, they also showed the incisions as they had been made by the surgeons and the pathway through the brain that they too to reach the points that needed to be operated on.

What does this have to do Autism and Asperger's Syndrome?

The answer to that is simple. There has been a lot of talk over the years that states that the Autism and Asperger's Syndrome brain are miswired, especially when compared to a Neurotypical brain. Now, we actually have the technology to actually map these neural paths and see if this is true. It turns out that I am not the only one who thinks so… Scientists have done it already.

Enter Temple Grandin. Dr. Grandin is famous. She is an Autist, writer, animal rights activist… and all around awesome person. Recently, Dr. Grandin had a High Definition Fiber Tracking scan done on herself. The results were… I would use the word conclusive, but that would require a lot more scans of a lot more Autists… But, the results were eye opening. The following image is a side by side comparison of Temple Grandin's brain (On the left) and a Neurotypical Brain (on the right).

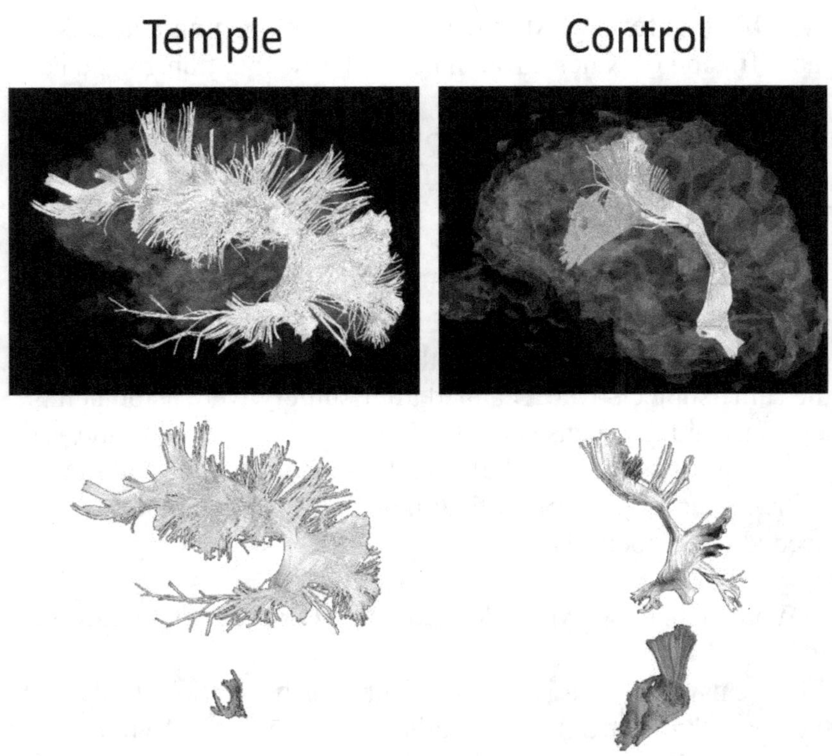

There is is… clear as day… Temple Grandin's brain is wired differently than the brain of a Neurotypical.

This technology is an amazing tool to learn about the physical causes of the mechanics of Autism. Some Autists are already stating that the technology has proven that the Autistic brain is different from the Neurotypical brain. We are a long way from conclusive proof. A long way. At this point, we have a

190

couple HDFT scans that hint at this.

For it to be conclusive, there needs to be many, many, many more scans taken. Eventually we will reach the point that we have conclusive proof that the autistic brain is wired completely different from NTs… Work is already being done to reach this goal. Further, studies are being conducted to see if there are differences between different types of Autistic Spectrum Disorders – High Functioning Autism, Low Functioning Autism, Asperger's…

I suspect that there are more types of Autism (based on the Neural Structures in the brain), than we know about thus far.

After looking at several different HDFT scans of Autistic brains, (which I've been doing all day in research for this article) I have noticed some things. The NT brain scans all seem to organize along the central axis of the brain, right between the hemispheres. The Autistic Spectrum Individual scans all seem to have similar structures, the major nerve tracts seem to be distributed across the brain relatively evenly…

While looking at these scans it reminded me of something else I had seen recently – a map of the internet and distributed computing networks across the globe…

38 – Boundaries and your Aspie

A lot of this series is based on personal experience – either things that I think people need to know, things people say to me, or questions I am asked. This part of the series is no different. Recently, I had the mother of an Autist tell me that Autistic Spectrum Individuals have problems respecting boundaries. She went on to tell me that I, as an Aspie, was incapable of respecting the boundaries as set forth by other people – that I was wired in such a way that it was not physically possible for me to do it.

I was offended… I was angry… and I was outraged… It's actually taken me a bit of time to get to the point where I can actually write about it without a rant.

Autistic Spectrum Individuals are more than capable of respecting other people's boundaries. As a matter of fact, the Autists I know are terribly conscious of boundaries and would rather take a bullet than violate them… When they KNOW about them.

Therein lies the problem.

Autistic Spectrum Individuals, whether they are low functioning, high functioning or Aspies, all have problems with realizing that there are boundaries to obey.

When an NT encounters a situation that has inherent (i.e. unspoken) rules and boundaries, they have the ability to intuitively know what these rules and boundaries are. That is part of the NT condition – being able to absorb the finer points of a social situation without effort. The NTs I know are unable to grasp the fact that we can't do that. It is such an intrinsic portion of their psyche that it is, to them, like breathing. So it is mystifying that we cannot do this.

As such, since this is so far out of their realm of understanding, they assume that we see these imaginary lines in the sand that surround us, and that we are intentionally crossing them. If this were the case, we'd all be sociopathic, not Autistic.

As astounding as it sounds – we REALLY don't see these boundaries. We don't perceive the unease we cause by our actions or words when we cross them. What seems ironic to me is that it is considered impolite to cross these boundaries… but it is just as impolite to call people out on boundary crossing. Simply put, calling someone on a boundary issue is a boundary. From where I stand, this is a silly boundary, a social construct and part of the social contract that needs to be abandoned.

No, this is not a case of asking for concessions because I have Asperger's. This is the Autistic Spectrum Community asking for you to make a concession to your own comfort. If the Autist in your life crosses a boundary, it is not because they see it and choose to ignore it… it is because they do not know better. AND they won't know any better unless someone tells them.

The issue is that most NTs don't explain what was done wrong in the terms of "Neurotypicals find >>>behavior A<<< offensive or uncomfortable because of >>>INSERT REASON<<<." They jump to the accusations… "Why would you do that?" The problem with questions like this is that the Autist does not even realize that the request for information indicates that an action violated the societal social contract. We often ask the same kind of questions when we want to understand the motives of another person or are confused by their words/actions (which is often).

If you really want to help your Autist learn social skills, training has to be done. To do this, you have to boil social situations down to their lowest common contributing factors. You have to remember that we don't grasp this stuff inherently or automatically and often need it spelled out for us.

An example is interrupting. Many Aspies and Autists will interrupt conversations. The reason for this is simple… We the NTs doing it constantly. What many of us don't realize is the interpersonal relationships that are at work in that group. We can't pick up on the subtle indicators that Brad and James are best friends, James and Monique are dating and Brad and Frank are dating. We can't, at a glance, see that these people are good friends. Therefore, we are not aware of what is acceptable for these friends vs. the general public. We only see what they are doing at that moment. So, when we interrupt the conversation to say something… we are violating their "This is how we act with each other" vs. "This is what we accept from outsiders." Social construct.

As such, what is needed is clear boundary training… For instance… you tell all of your friends that your Autist doesn't enjoy being hugged or touched by strangers… You are drawing a line in the sand for them. Why is it so hard to do the same for your Autist?

A couple examples:
Hand Flapping – "Just so you know, when you get agitated, you flap your hands. NTs view this as a warning sign. It makes them uneasy because they sense that something is wrong and when one of them does it, it reflects an unstable mental state. They expect an outburst of grief, anger or something equally unpleasant. Just remember that, and if they are concerned, explain your condition to them."

Special Interests – "You and I both know that you are excited about >>>special interest<<<, but unless they want to know more about it, talking about it for hours makes them think you are arrogant and uninterested in their interests or what they have to say."

If someone had taken the time to explain these boundaries and the REASONS WHY, my life would have been so much easier.

I spent the first 20 years of my life thinking everyone around me was actively hostile for this very reason. I thought that people were baring their teeth at me, like animals do when threatened, when they were smiling. Then, one day, The Bean caught on to what was happening. She explained to me that these were smiles – Honest expressions of joy and happiness. This was an eye opener for me… I REALLY didn't know that was what they were doing.

This, as with so much when dealing with Autistic Spectrum Individuals, hinges on communication. When your Autist asks about an event that confuses them, they are actually asking for a why… Why did this happen. Why did the NTs react like this? Why do they think I am weird, rude, arrogant… Try to analyze the situation for hidden social boundaries that your Autist may have missed and explain them… Try to explain it in the format of – "NTs behave like >>>INSERT BEHAVIOR<<<, so when you do >>>INSERT BEHAVIOR<<< – they feel >>>INSERT REACTION<<<. You might want to try >>>ALTERNATIVE BEHAVIOR<<<." There will be slip ups when your Autist treats the rules as absolute and misses the exceptions and modifiers to social interactions, but those can be explained as well.

The following is a description of anxiety according to the May Clinic:

"Anxiety happens as a normal part of life. It can even be useful when it alerts you to danger. But for some people, anxiety persistently interferes with daily activities such as work, school or sleep. This type of anxiety can disrupt relationships and enjoyment of life, and over time it can lead to health concerns and other problems."

Anxiety is a part of the normal response to fear and danger. It is something that we inherited from our ancestors (whether they be cro-magnon man, cave men, or monkeys) and is a natural function of mind and body in the Neurotypical brain and body. This is, of course, when it is functioning properly.

I have written about it before in my piece of co-morbid conditions and Asperger's Syndrome, but I think that the subject could use a few more words thrown at it. You see, everyone experiences anxiety from time to time… but your Autist will, most likely, experience it more often than the NTs around you. It is a part of every day life for Aspies and often, our pet NTs will dismiss it as us just being nervous or upset about something in our life.

I would like to take a moment to put it into perspective for you. You, as an NT have had an anxious moment or two in your life. Think about that time you were out after dark and you heard that sound that you couldn't identify… That moment before you are truly frightened – that is anxiety. When your hair stands on end, your heart thunders, you start breathing rapidly and shallowly, and start sweating… That is the moment of anxiety before your fight or flight instinct kicks in.

That is anxiety… It's unpleasant, and many Autists live with it every day.

What is odd about this is that there are many stories about Aspies and Autists being fearless in dangerous situations. This next statement is merely supposition on my part – I believe that we have a malfunctioning fight or flight reflex. I don't think it kicks in when it is supposed to. I also don't think that it kicks in when it would be advantageous. The fight or flight reflex releases neurological pressure that builds up in the psyche. Without this pressure release, all that is left is the anxiety without anywhere to go.

As I stated in a previous issue of this series:
"Anxiety Disorders are a common problem for Autistic Spectrum individuals. Most anxiety disorders aren't diagnosed in Autistic Spectrum individuals. The reason for this is that the symptomology of Anxiety Disorders over laps and can be explained by the Autism diagnosis itself." Anxiety Disorders may be indicated by some or all of the following symptoms:
- Feelings of panic, fear, and uneasiness
- Uncontrollable, obsessive thoughts
- Repeated thoughts or flashbacks of traumatic experiences
- Nightmares
- Ritualistic behaviors, such as repeated hand washing
- Problems sleeping
- Cold or sweaty hands and/or feet
- Shortness of breath
- Palpitations
- An inability to be still and calm
- Dry mouth
- Numbness or tingling in the hands or feet
- Nausea
- Muscle tension
- Dizziness

Anxiety Disorders have been reported to occur in between 11% and 84% of Autism Spectrum individuals. The wide range in this case is due to differences in methodology of studies."

It all sounds familiar, doesn't it? That's because your Autist suffers from anxiety but doesn't have the vocabulary to adequately explain what is going on in their head. And without the pressure relief valve of Fight or Flight, that anxiety builds.

It has to go somewhere… Sometimes it can be expressed as laughter (inappropriate laughter in the case of Autists) as discussed HERE. Other times, it just comes out as frustration, spastic motion, hand flapping, outbursts or meltdowns.

I have been told by several of the female NT friends that sometimes they need to work out, take a walk, or just dance. My male friends will spar with me (martial arts is something I have been practicing my entire adult life), lift weights or play video games… All of these thing provide a pressure release for the NTs in question.

With the mis-wiring of the Autist brain, it becomes very difficult to let this anxious energy dissipate. Due to the neural tracts being so diversified through the Aspie brain, as revealed with High Definition Fiber Tracking and discussed HERE – at times, anxiety can and does seem completely sourceless to the Autist. As with NTs the energy has to dissipate some way.

When you look at the unfocused nature of the neural tracts it is easy to see why the releases of neural energy that are necessary to rid the mind of anxiety are not the same in your Autist as they are in NTs. Laughter, outbursts, yelling, flapping hands… these things are necessary for the mental health of your Autist. Let them happen.

Speaking as someone who tried to restrain these actions and behaviors for almost a decade… they ARE necessary… Since I had no other way to work out my anxiety…I had a complete mental breakdown that I almost didn't recover from. It put me in a mental hospital for 8 weeks and did a great deal of damage.

So, please… let us vent in the only way we can. You get to… don't keep us from doing it.

40 – Self Diagnostics; where do I go from here?

With the prevalence of Autistic Spectrum Disorders, one needs to know… Often, adults with Autistic Spectrum Disorders or Asperger's will suspect that there is something wrong. They will feel it in their bones. They will see the bewildered looks others give them in social situations and know something is wrong. They will find themselves overwhelmed in these same situations, or by sensory input, and they will just know that something is not right… not right inside…

I have stated, quite often, that self diagnosis is not a diagnosis at all. I have taken a lot of heat for my stance on that. I have been called a bully an ass and ignorant for my stance. One response was a direct comment on my blog.

"…what you say here is just wrong. I found out about Asperger's almost be accident, researched it myself, then got a diagnosis – I certainly would not have got this if I had not done all the leg work myself! You have no right to put down people – many who have struggled all their lives with these symptoms – who have found out about this condition themselves and have the courage to face it. This is arrogant and I am afraid downright ignorant!"

I stick by the statement, but I believe, due to the nature of the response that it has provoked, that I need to explain a little bit.

It seems that my words have been interpreted as "Self diagnosis is useless." Which has never been my intent. I believe that self diagnosis is an important and integral part of the diagnostic process. Based on the opinion of mental health professionals (and not just one, but many of them – and I have worked in the psychiatric field for quite a while), self-diagnosis is the FIRST step. The individual has used layman's tools to confirm (in their own mind) that they have an Autism Spectrum Disorder… but using these tools is not the same as a diagnosis.

Often, people stop there – and that is where I start to take issue with them.

There are a few reasons for this. Self diagnostics are an important step in the process, but a diagnosis by definition can only be made by a medial professionals. According to the Science Dictionary diagnosis is:
"The identification by a medical provider of a condition, disease, or injury made by evaluating the symptoms and signs presented by a patient."

There are other reasons as well. Let's talk about treatment. There are comorbid conditions, and some symptoms that can be treated with medication. To procure medication, one needs to have a diagnosis… from a MEDICAL PROFESSIONAL.

Medical Professionals train for 12 years to practice in their chosen fields. 4 years for their bachelors degree, 4 years in med school, and then 4 years in residency… This training is what makes them uniquely qualified to grant a diagnosis. The reason that a diagnosis is so very important is treatment. Treatment plans are tailored to the specific individual and are completely dependent on their… you guessed it… their diagnosis.

Diagnostic criteria often overlap… What does that mean? It means that many different conditions, diseases, and syndromes can and do have similar diagnostic traits. If you don't believe me, go to the diagnostic tool on webMD some time and try to diagnose something… ANYTHING… it will be a range of thing… a fungal infection, a spider bite and CANCER… tuberculosis, the flue and CANCER… And that is why an official diagnosis is so very important.

Misdiagnosis can be dangerous. Bipolar can be misdiagnosed as Asperger's. Some of the medications used to treat the anxiety issues associated with Asperger's Syndrome can cause suicidal thoughts and tendencies, mania and hyper-manic episodes… All of which can be dangerous to the patient and those around them. It can actually cause brain damage. Further, the the cognitive behavioral training required for normalization and socialization of Autistic Spectrum Individuals needs to be tailored to the individual. If the wrong treatment program is applied (as is common in a self diagnosis or misdiagnosis), it can really screw a person up… just like with the wrong medication for the wrong condition.

These two things (12 years of formal training and the dangers of misdiagnosis) are why I insist that self diagnosis is NOT an actual diagnosis… As I have stated… and will state again… self-diagnosis is not a diagnosis at all… BUT IT IS AN IMPORTANT STEP… If you have a self diagnosis, then you NEED to seek a psychiatric professional to give you a diagnosis so that you can move forward with confidence and get the needed treatment.

To that end… I recommend the following site for self diagnosis.
http://rdos.net/eng/Aspie-quiz.php

For the record… my scores:
Your Aspie score: 191 of 200
Your neurotypical (non-autistic) score: 13 of 200
You are very likely an Aspie

This is a useful tool for self diagnosis. If you take this test and it comes out positive… please… PLEASE get a diagnosis so that you can start treatment, counseling, socialization or normalization…

Isn't that really the goal? I mean… really? Why bother with a self diagnosis if you are not working to make your life better?

I have been writing this series under a conception that was fostered by the basic classification of Asperger's Syndrome. In the DSM, it has been listed as an Autistic Spectrum Disorder. And, as such, I have been approaching it from that precept… that Asperger's and Autism are different manifestations of the same physical issues.

I have even gotten into several very heated discussions… No, that's not right…I have gotten into the forum equivalent of screaming, hair pulling, knock down, drag out, fights over this point. I stuck by my guns… simply because that was the classification – an Autistic Spectrum Disorder. And that is, honestly, part of Asperger's–obsession with technicalities and parts of things. Since it was classified as an Autistic Spectrum Disorder… that's what it was. But it was only classified as such because we really didn't know any better.

Recently, I wrote a piece about High Definition Fiber Tracking and Temple Grandin's Brain vs. a Neurotypical Brain. There were marked differences in the physical structure of NT and her Autistic Brain.

There is another technique that is being applied to research into Asperger's Syndrome and Autism. It is known as an Active or Functional Magnetic Resonance Imaging scan. An article about it says the following:

"Functional Magnetic Resonance Imaging (fMRI) is a type of MRI that allows you to see which parts of your brain are active when you perform different tasks or feel certain emotions and sensations. Brain activity requires energy and a good supply of oxygen-rich blood. The scanner can see the increase in blood flow to the most active parts of the brain because it can detect the difference between hydrogen nuclei in oxygenated blood and those in de-oxygenated blood. In this way the scanner

builds-up a 3D map of which parts of the brain are working particularly hard. fMRI mapping of the brain is used to find out how the brain carries out mental tasks and what parts of the brain are responsible for different brain disorders."

Basically, the MRI scanner is used in real time (Thanks to a huge bump in computing power in recent years) to see where the blood is flowing in the brain. I haven't done any research into it, but I am going to assume that it is either by tracking the water or the iron in the blood, but I could be completely wrong about it.

Recent studies have compared fMRI scans of Autistic and Asperger's brains. These scans show that the processes associated with both conditions are different… and distinct. Meaning that Asperger's Syndrome and Autism MAY have the same root cause, but it manifests in a difference in the structures of the brain. Though, for the purposes of this discussion, the causes don't matter… regardless of the cause, the fact is that the studies are showing consistently, that Asperger's and Autistic brains are functioning differently…

I have a couple issues with this. The main issue that I have is in on my end. It puts a kink in my think… Since I have spent the last 20+ years under the assumption … no, that's not the right word. I was told for 20+ years by professionals that Asperger's and Autism are different aspects of the same physical condition. As this research progresses, I may have to re-evaluate everything I know about Autism and Asperger's.

The implications of the research are staggering. Provided that the structures of the brain are consistent within the two conditions, it will be possible to PHYSICALLY test for Autism and Asperger's Syndrome. It means that with fMRI and High Definition Fiber Tracking there will be no ambiguity in diagnosis. Everyone can be given a specific and accurate diagnosis every time.

However… as the HDFT scan of Temple Grandin's brain showed… The condition (of Autism, at least) is inherent. It can't be fixed. The nerve pathways, at least at today's level of technology and for the foreseeable future, cannot be rewritten… It's not as simple as brain surgery (I know… that is the definition of irony, isn't it – simple brain surgery)… it would be a complete rebuild from the ground up… like rebuilding a classic car from all original parts, only with materials that die within 5 minutes of oxygen deprivation.

It opens up a lot of possibilities for diagnosis and treatment… and also would free us from uncertainty (and hopefully prove my theory that there is a huge tendency to over diagnose) and clear up a lot of issues with ambiguity of symptomology.

42 – Sometimes… I fail at being a human being

The following statements about species, genetics and the like are not based in fact and are really only intended to drive home the point. I used to simply let hyperbole stand, but it seems that wasn't working… people did not seem to catch onto the fact that it was hyperbole for this reason… or that it was hyperbolic in nature at all… without further ado:

I know that you have noticed that your Aspie acts odd at the best of times… and downright weird at other times. It might help you to realize that your Aspie is actually a different species. NTs, Autistics and NTs (as studies are showing) have drastically different brain structures… This means, literally, that we are all drastically different in cognitive process and that you can't hold Autistics and Aspies to the same standards of communication and interaction that you do with NTs.

And the same sentiment can be applied across the board. What this means is that Autistics and Aspies have to make the same accommodations for NTs. They cannot be expected to communicate on the same level as we do any more than we can be expected to communicate on theirs.

I guess that I shouldn't have even used the word level as it bears the connotations that I am trying to avoid. And by level, I am not talking about intellectual capacity. I am not talking about intelligence. I am not stating that anyone is better than anyone else. I probably should have used the word plane. We exist on different planes… at certain places, these planes of thought intersect, allowing us the semblance of communication. Unfortunately, due to the inherent differences between brain structures, social skills, thought processes and mental conditioning, this communication is nothing more than a veneer.

I know I have been harping on a specific scanning process

called High Definition Fiber Tracking and a specific image recently, but it really is an important image… Here it is again.

Temple   Control

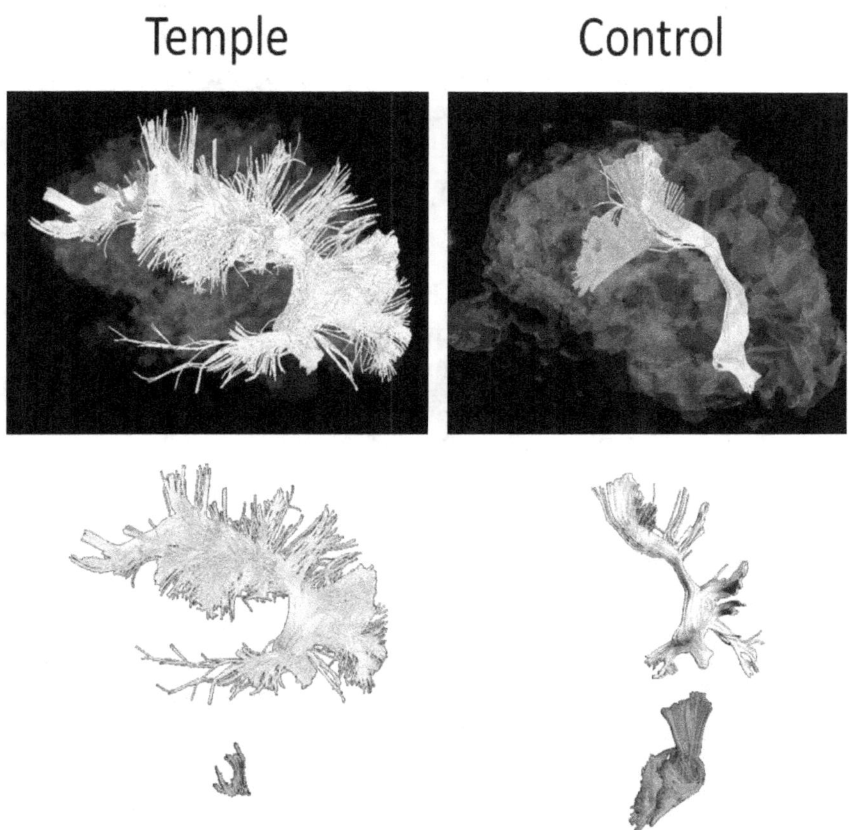

Look at that. Take a good, long look… That is an Autisic brain next to an NT brain. Is it little wonder that we are on different planes when attempting to communicate? When the HDFT scans of Aspie brains come back, I suspect we will see similar, but different diversification of Neural Tracks in the brain. We already have some basic studies showing that the Asperger's Brain and the Autistic Brain when using Functional MRI scans during comparable stimuli.

In simple terms, NTs, Autistics, and Aspies all have completely different brains. That means that they process information, input, stimuli, language, emotions and cognition in completely different ways. They are as different as different species of primates. That's right… there is as much (if not more) difference between Aspie, NT and Autistic Brains as there are between chimps, gorillas and bonobos… (NO… I am not saying who is what… that would be offensive to all involved).

In the case of Autistics, fMRI scans have been showing relatively consistent results in the working patterns of the brain. Provided that the results continue being consistent and that fMRI scans reveal that Autistics all have the same functionality to their cognitive processes… So… we have three very different brain structures, and recent findings are linking Autism and Asperger's to specific sets of genes… we basically have three very similar, but distinctly different species here on the planet Earth.

And therein, honestly, lies the problem. When an NT hears a specific word – certain parts of their brain will activate and light up in the fMRI scans. In the fMRIs, different parts of Autistic Brains light up with the same words. And, as studies progress, I suspect that Aspie fMRI scans will show that still different sections of the brain are active with identical words and identical stimuli.

So, the root of the problem, really is that we all process words differently… it's not even a case of misinterpretation of words, or a lack of knowledge of the definitions of the words themselves… It is an inherent difference in processing. Since an NT has regions a, b, and c light up when he hears the word Dog; Autistics have sections a, q, and p light up when they hear the same word; and Aspies have regions f, t and "oh look! a kitty!"

light up at the same word – the associations, processing, and cognitive flavors are all going to be different for all of them. Not only that, but the cognitive dissonance required for decision making processes are different as well.

Autistics have described words as soft, or cold, or prickly. Aspies (myself included) have described words as bitter, metallic, or spicy. I've never heard that kind of description from NTs… That is not to say that they don't…but I have asked and most of them say that they don't process words that way.

With these differences in cognitive processes, communication can be a challenge. Throughout this series, I have been urging the NTs to allow and adjust for differences in communication, but it really goes farther than that. We are all different. It may be a case of one functionality is right and the others or broken -or- it may be that all are just different… but since we all process words, images, sounds and other stimuli differently, we all have to make adjustments and take some time to find a common frame of reference for one another… Also, we should have some patience when dealing with our companions on this terrestrial starship called Earth.

With effort from all sides, we can mange meaningful communication. The upshot of this is that Autistics and Aspies are OFTEN baffled by NT attempts to communicate. Hell… we are often confused by our OWN attempts to communicate. Personally, as an Aspie, I have been working on adapting and blending with NT society. I fail… often… but these studies are giving me a new frame of reference… I am not failing so much at being a human being… I am succeeding, more often than not, at finding a frame of reference between very different species.

43 – There is no way that is me!

I came to a realization the other day. Before I wrote about it, I did some inquiring and some research. I've been struggling with this piece all day… It's mainly because I cannot find a name for what I want to discuss. At first, I thought that it fit under the heading of Body Dysmorphic Disorder… but that wasn't it.

I was in the bathroom today and I caught sight of my own reflection in the mirror… and for a moment, I was shocked… I looked at it and was actually confused by what I saw. My brain could not rectify the guy in the mirror with who I am. I asked the sister person (if you don't remember – she is Autistic), a couple Aspie acquaintances, and asked some people on one of the Autistic spectrum boards… and it seems that this is common.

There was a term for it in the movie – "The Matrix." They called it "residual self image." It was explained as the way a person sees themselves. It's odd… because one's self image can be DRASTICALLY different than the reality of the situation. I don't know about NTs, but Autistics and Aspies can look in the mirror and never really see the whole of what is in that mirror.

This may sound odd to the average NT, but I brush my teeth, shave my face and groom my goatee and mustache routinely… but I never see myself… Not really… I see the parts, but never the whole. Not really. And, honestly, that is part of the diagnostics for Autism and Asperger's… Obsession of the parts of things. This obsession over the parts of things, has a downside… ignorance of the whole.

One way (at least for me) that this manifests is that I really don't realize how big I am. In case I haven't mentioned it… I am 6'9"… that's right…I am over 2 meters tall. I weigh in at 295 pounds (134 kg). I am a MONSTER of a man… The thing is, I don't realize it. Even after seeing it, over and over and over… I don't realize how I must appear to other people…I never see it until I see myself in photos with other… normal people. And when I do see the pics of me with other people… it is a shock… every time… EVERY time.

Why am I discussing this here? Well… Many NTs have commented that their Autistics and Aspies seem very down on themselves… That they cannot comprehend why someone would want to be our friend, or why someone would be attracted to us. And the answer is this dysmorphic view of ourselves, this residual self image that has nothing to do with how we really look or who we are intellectually.

You will find that your Autist or Aspie will have problems accepting compliments that do not align with their own perceptions of why they are. A lot of people take this to mean that we have low self esteem, but that is not the case at all. It is that we have a very firm and concrete image of who we are, of what we look like. True, this image is often wrong… Often DRAMATICALLY wrong, but it is what we KNOW about ourselves.

That is why compliments often make your Autist or Aspie uncomfortable. We cannot imagine why someone would make a statement that is so obviously not in= keeping with what we know about ourselves.

And this can be a big deal in many, many situations – compliments on appearance, especially from a romance interest, since most of us don't see ourselves as the object of romantic interest; compliments on skill sets; compliments on achievement; artistic achievement… Just keep in mind that we don't see ourselves the same way you do… so giving us a compliment may be a difficult task. But ALSO watch out… we can be terribly arrogant about those thing we KNOW about ourselves.

44 – What's with all this junk?

Before you read this piece, I KNOW that hoarding is not
exclusively with Autism Spectrum Disorders or Asperger's
Syndrome… HOWEVER, Autistic Spectrum Disorders in
general and Asperger's Syndrome specifically are marked by
obsessive tendencies and "Special Interests."

Anyone that has had any hobbies knows that there is STUFF
that goes along with it. Every hobby has certain accouterments
associated with EVERY hobby. Painters need frames, easels,
paints and brushes; Table Top Gamers have books, books, more
books, dice and notes; console gamers have consoles,
controllers, games and peripherals; make up artists have
molding materials, casting materials, paints, glues and sculpting
materials; bibliophiles have ALL the books. They all have their
junk. The clutter associated with any one hobby can be a bit
much.

We all have hobbies, so you understand. Now… imagine
picking up a new hobby 3 or four times a year. Sometimes more
often than that. You hear about something, or read about it and
it seizes your imagination… Then you research. Then you do.
You do… A LOT… and to do… you have to buy the gear and
materials for this new hobby… all of it… Then you reach a
passable skill level and are proud of your work… and then…
AND THEN… a NEW special interest takes hold and you move
on…

Why do we do that?

Well… It has to do with the release of endorphins, stimulus
and diminishing returns. I discuss it in a lot more depth HERE.

Now… I have said it before, but it bears repeating… Most
Aspies go from obsessive interest to obsessive interest… but

some lucky few of us find interests that become life long SPECIAL INTERESTS! I am one of those lucky few… and I STILL have passing interests on top of everything. Since I am the only one I can speak about with any amount of certainty.

I have several major lifelong interests…
1. video games
2. remote control vehicles
3. action figures
4. film making/photography
5. Costuming

Video games require a lot of space… I have a gaming PC, a ps2, a ps 3, an X-box 360 and a 55 inch TV. I have 2-4 controllers for each of these, an ethernet switch, memory cards, cables, adapters, controller extensions, and hundreds of game disks. I WANT a gamecube, an original X-box and a dream cast.

My action figures are (mostly video gamer oriented). I have a thing for Iron Man, so I have a few Iron Man Figures (Including a couple plushies). I have a lot of halo figures and vehicles, a Naughty Bear, some minions, some stuff from Gears of War, ALL THE SKYLANDERS, Nathan Drake and Cole McGrath. These are on shelves over my TV, and above the couch and a display case.

I have an RC truck, two quadcopter drones, a small model hovercraft, a couple RC helicopters and a couple of Halo RC vehicles.

My costuming requires brushes, boxes of tools, card, warblo, paints, glues, scissors, leatherworking materials, dyes, card, casting supplies, make-up…

And my photography/film making has cameras, mics, tripods, lights, booms, a jib, a desktop computer, a laptop, Go Pro

Cameras, gig bags for lights, a green screen, vest and steadicam… and LOTS of other little things…

Just think about all of this stuff… These are JUST my PERMANENT SPECIAL INTERESTS. So… expect your Aspie to have a lot of junk. These things are ALL necessary for our interests… We already feel weird about it… but we have no choice… this stimulus helps us feel… it helps us feel good… and we have no other choice. We have to do it… so admire it… revel in it… especially when we tell you about it. The fact that we are sharing this part of our life with you means that you are a very special person and we trust you.

Sometimes it is completely appropriate to be impolite.
No, Seriously. Politeness, at times is an affront to one's true feelings. If you are in a situation where politeness would TRULY be damaging to self esteem, cause excessive dissonance or psychological damage… Then it is appropriate, allowable and NECESSARY to eschew politeness. This is a form of standing up for yourself.

I am not advocating that you use this as carte blanche to be an ass. Only use this when it is necessary. You are Autistic/Aspie… sometimes, you get a buy. What is important here is that we have to take care of ourselves before we can take care of anything else…

Keep your eyes open.
Seriously… pat attention to what's going on around you. We have a tendency to hide in a corner and ignore those things that do not agree with our personal paradigm. This is a bad idea. You miss a lot, and can alienate those around you… Specifically, those who support you.

When life gives you a lemon, say 'Lemons? I like lemons. What else have you got?
Everybody says "Make lemonade." We are designed to think differently… Do it. Often, conforming to a societal expectation is a bad idea. If you like lemons, take the lemons. If you don't like lemons, send them back. Lemonade is bad for you anyway.

Beware of all enterprises that require new clothes.
Seriously… if you have a wardrobe that you are comfortable in, don't stray from it. If you take a job, or a social event that forces you into a different wardrobe, you will be uncomfortable in it. What's funny is that (most of the time) NTs can't read us at all, but if we are uncomfortable, their lizard brain will pick up

on it and they will be completely unable to be comfortable in our presence. Stay within your comfort zone… NO MATTER WHAT.

All the technologies you take for granted were created by living, breathing, thinking, dreaming human beings just like you.

The reason I tell you this is because all things are possible with creativity, power and ingenuity… and you have it. So, don't EVER let them get you down. You are intelligent, powerful and see things from a different perspective… Use these traits… NEVER STOP using these traits.

The reason people get lost in thought is because it is, to many, rather unfamiliar territory.
Most people don't think. They are not designed for it. I know this sounds cruel… but it is accurate. The human animal is designed to survive on instinct alone. We have gotten past our roots and live in a world that requires thought… since most are not equipped for it, it is hard for them. Aspies, on the whole, think a lot more than the average human being. Take a moment to realize that they don't… get over it and move on.

A truly wise man never plays leapfrog with a Unicorn.
Often, with a little forethought, we can see what is coming up. Life consists of a series of happenings… Cause, effect, effect. If you think about what you are doing… think two steps up the chain, we can prevent the truly painful events in our life. So… think and don't jump into stupid situations and you won't get stabbed in the butt.

Being proud of how many books you've read is the surest sign you haven't read nearly enough.
Achieve. Always strive to be better. Do better, make something of yourself, learn… always keep learning… But

don't brag about it. No matter how much you learn. No matter how much you do, there is always someone out there that is smarter than you and will have done more than you.

No man is an island, but then no man is a potato salad, either.

Everyone tries to tell us that we need to be social. That we can't exist alone… we have to have a social group, have to go out and do something, go out and be with people… Most times, they use the old adage, "No man is an island." Well, I'm not a potato salad… or a box, chopped liver or Luc Beson… or a crouton. Well…I might be a crouton – all quanta being equal, I can't tell… but I don't know what any of that has to do with anything… So… be an island if you want… or a crouton… I REALLY think we're all croutons.

"Opportunity is missed by most people because it is dressed in overalls and looks like work." ~Thomas Edison

Anything worth having is worth working for. Plain and simple. So many people spend their lives waiting for it to "happen to them." Screw that. It only happens through perseverance… when opportunity knocks, grab a shovel, put on your work boots and SWEAT.

46 – Are you going to let them… erm, you talk to you like that?

Today, I spent a lovely afternoon with a close friend of mine. We've been talking about doing a photo shoot for the last few months. We finally got the time and were able to synchronize our schedules to get it done. While we were shooting, Nyx and I were talking, and something horrible came to light. This beautiful, strong and powerful woman has little to no self esteem.

We talked about it… a lot… And she has her reasons… they were all wrong… but she had them. And it got me thinking. Almost every Aspie I know has problems with self esteem and I am not sure why.

In spite of the fact that we are socially awkward, odd and think in a different way than NTs do, most Aspies are attractive, lovable and capable… but for some reason, we don't see it in ourselves.

But this is only one aspect of the issue… I have been sitting here for about an hour trying to figure out how to explain it… and honestly, this is the only thing I can come up with.

For those of you who have problems with lyrics and music… here are the pertinent lyrics…

"There are so many vampires, inside, outside, and nationwide,
it helps to recognize them with this vampire hunting guide!
Listen closely, a vampire is any person or thought or feeling
that stands between you and your creative self expression,
but they can assume many seductive forms.
…
First up are you pygmy vampires.

Take out the part about creative self expression and insert you
and a general feeling of well being. These are the things that
interfere with happiness, because when you have low self
esteem, you can't be completely happy even when everything is
working out for you.

Ironically enough, I am having vampire problems as I try to
write this piece… It is coming out clumsy and rambling…

Yes… Let's get to the point.

So… I'll get to the point. When it comes to self esteem, our
worst enemy resides in our head. No matter how brilliant,
attractive and overall awesome we are, someone in our head
tells us the exact opposite… and the problem is, we listen to
them. We let this little voice inside our head tell us these vile

things, destroy what value we place on our own intellect, instincts… hell… our soul…

And all of this brings me to my point. Honestly, if someone walked up to me on the street and said some of the things that I say to my self, I would slap them across the face. So… We won't take it from others… why the hell do we let ourselves destroy us? No… don't answer… Think about it. Seriously think about it. Why? Seriously, I can't even begin to answer it.

So… every time you wake up… remember IALAC… I Am Lovable And Capable. Hold that close and don't let it go. In spite of the Aspie tendency towards being disgusted in our skill level when we don't succeed immediately at something new; in spite of the vampires chewing on our brain; in spite of our tendency towards self loathing… We are lovable and capable…

Chant it… Live it… IALAC.

If you are romantically involved with an Aspie, it can be difficult to find things to do on dates. I can speak from experience… I am kind of difficult to deal with at the best of times. I am surprised and thankful that my female friends want anything to do with me, let alone enjoy hanging out with me. Most of the time, NTs want to "do things" or "go out." In short, they want to take their Aspie out of the comfort zone and that can be horrifying and dissonant for any Aspie.

Why is that, you ask?

Well… Most Aspies, over time, develop an aversion to stressful and uncertain social situations. Some of us develop full blown anxiety, or even panic over these situations… Let me tell you a little about why.

Let's say you want to go to a bar and take your Aspie with you. To you, a bar is a place to enjoy some music, grab an alcoholic beverage, meet new people and relax. To your Aspie, a bar is drastically different place. First off… IT'S LOUD. The music is loud, the people are loud… Even if your Aspie doesn't have sensory issues, it is a wall of sound that presses on your chest and is very unnerving. We are very sensitive to sensory stimuli and rely on it to take in the world. If we can't hear anything beyond the loud, blaring music and yelling people… we can't accurately experience the environment.

Further… there are some pretty heinous scents in a bar. I have spoken to my NT friends, and they don't notice them… but I do… And I REALLY don't know how they can't smell it. I used to work at a bar. The bar had several distinctive smells to it in layers. First off is alcohol… No matter how well the staff cleans the bar, they can't get rid of that smell. To do so would require shampooing the carpet in the bar nightly. As the alcohol evaporates, the sugars and water in the drinks soak into the carpet and there is the faint smell of wet carpet, mildew and mold. Then there is the bathroom smell… Drunk people piss on the wall, the floor and more… this soaks into baseboards and plaster… no amount of cleaning will remove that faint smell of urine. Lastly… smoke… stale smoke lingers in every crevice of the place… And THAT is just an empty bar… add people actively smoking, loud music, people yelling and being packed in so tight that people are always TOUCHING YOU!

Really… I don't know how you can do it. I know one Aspie that routinely goes to live music venues because one of her special interests is photographing live events. She has some problems with the noise, lights and people, but can do it. I am impressed that she can…I know I can't.

There are many other places that NTs want to go… and most of them are problematic (at best) for your Aspie. I'm not going to go into them, because that's really self defeating in the grand scheme of things. So… let's look at the reality of the situation. In all probability, your Aspie is a bit of a recluse, and if they are not. They have specific places they want to go.

These are places that they feel comfortable with – home, a beautiful spot on the river, a favorite shop, or a specific restaurant. While we can be acclimated to a new location with some work, you need to remember that these places are the ones we've worked on. By inviting you share them with us, we are showing you an incredible amount of trust… which, for a lot of us is hard to give, especially to NTs.

Most of us are willing to experiment, to try new things and places, but you gotta work with us… but first… try going to our places. Try seeing what we see, why we like them… there is a simple beauty in it all.

48 – Aren't We All Just a Little Autistic?

There is a question that I have encountered a number of times that bothers me. "Aren't we all just a little Autistic?" I hold nothing against the people that ask this… As a matter of fact, several that have asked me that are good friends of mine.

But I have to say that the answer is No. No we aren't.

In the past, I have been glib in my response to it, and I am sure I have hurt some feelings… but it is frustrating… if we were all a little Autistic, then Autists and Aspies would be the norm…we'd be the NTs and the Irrational Feelies (IFs for short) would be the odd ones, not us.

So… I have to say no… no… a thousand times no.

A friend of mine states that a lot of people have strong autistic perceptions. I've actually heard this phrase a couple times, but have never really explored it. I have tried on several occasions to research it… but have failed to wrap my mind around it.

I have to say, this… if you feel you have Autistic or Aspie tendencies, then there are two possibilities (as I see it).
1. you ARE an Aspie or Autistic.

2. As an NT, your empathy is probably tricking you into thinking that you have these traits and is unaware of what it is really like.

I know, some people are offended by this, but that is not the intent… and honestly, if you are offended by the statement, I can truthfully say that it is unlikely that you are one of us.

HOWEVER… if you are plagued by "Autistic Perceptions"

and are convinced that it is not a case of Empathy, then the next thing you NEED to do is start on the path of Diagnosis. The first step on that path is self diagnosis... If you have the perceptions of an Autist, then you really need to be sure... You need to know. Why? Well... Knowing is half the battle... right?

The aspie test I mentioned earlier in this book is a good bench mark. It is by NO MEANS an actual diagnosis... that requires a health care professional. But go ahead... take test. I'll wait because this is important. What did you score? If you scored over 32... There is a good chance that you are Autistic or an Aspie...

Why does it matter? Well... honestly, I have struggled my entire life with the issues that accompany my Asperger's Syndrome. Literally, it is a struggle every day. It may be overly emotional and irrational, but when someone claims to be partially Autistic/Aspie or, for that matter, completely Autistic/Aspie – it seems that they are minimizing my personal experiences and struggles. I know that is not their intent... but it is how it all feels.

As such... I will always answer "No." to that question. I try not to draw a line in the sand between NT and Autist, but it's already there. Fortunately, there are methods to determine which side of the line you are on. Fortunately, we are all thinking beings... and the line does not require that we throw down... only that we acknowledge our beautiful differences.

49 – OH MY GOD!!! SHUT UP AND STOP INTERRUPTING ME!!!

This is one of those entries I have been putting off for a while… And the reason for it is that it kind of puts us in a negative light. There are two sides to the issue, really…

Interrupting conversations… We do it. Unless it is a group of close friends or family, it is my understanding that NTs see interruptions as a form of disrespect. I have been told that NTs see conversational interruptions as a way of saying, "I don't care what you have to say." Sometimes, this is true – but not often.

Honestly, when dealing with an Aspie, conversational interruptions are not intended to be disrespectful. I have spoken to several Aspies on the subject, and (Of the Aspies who I polled) interruption is just something that happens. When we interrupt, it is not because we disrespect you, or don't care what you think… When we have thoughts, they often come in a rush… they flood into our head in a scene reminiscent of any breaking dam scene in any disaster film you have ever scene…

Think about that analogy… we process information in a different manner, and when we come to our conclusions, they burst the dam and flood into our brain. Like with that metaphorical flood, the thoughts move with the force of a battering ram… they hit, bounce around and keep moving… If we don't get them out when they strike, they can be swept away from us in the rush of mental pressure…

When thoughts are fleeting, we often fear that we will lose our ability to be understood, so when we have a thought, we have to get it out. That being said, with practice, we can learn to latch on to those thoughts and hang onto them long enough to be polite.

And honestly, most of the time, we don't even realize that
we're doing it. So, the best way to discourage the behavior is a
reminder... Don't get angry when it happens, just point it out...
talk to your Aspie about it and, between the two of you, work
out a code word between the two of you. Something that you
can say to them to remind them that they are doing it. With
awareness of a behavior comes the ability to modify said
behaviors.

A great many of our social problems are a result of
interruption. Many NTs get very upset with it, and as such,
mastering the art of conversational restraint is an attainable
goal.

This, however, is a double edged sword. NTs, as they get into
a relationship (and by this I mean romance, family, or
friendship), will start to feel more comfortable with the
situation. As they do, they will do what friends do, which means
they will interrupt. It's something that groups of NTs will do.
Often, that is the way a social group of NTs interact – they all
speak over one another and (because they are friends) they
interrupt each other... and this is the status quo.

Now... remember how our thoughts come – a flood of
words... To be able to speak, we often have to wrestle with our
thoughts. It is like grappling with the greased up deaf guy from
Family Guy.

So, we work hard to speak... grabbing those thoughts and
forcing them into a semblance of order. Once we have them in
order, we start to speak. If we are interrupted, our thoughts tend
to get jumbled again. So, we have to start the thought over.

You will find that, in these situations, the NTs will be
laughing, talking over each other and having a good time and

your Aspie will say the same 4-8 words… over and over and over again. It's because they are starting their thought and getting interrupted, having to start the thought over.

Remember what I said about how NTs view interruptions… a lack of respect and conveying the impression that you don't care about what they have to say? Well… The first couple times, your Aspie just accepts it… this is the way NTs are… and many of us understand that we do it, too… and turn about is fair play.

After the 4th or 5th time, we start to get upset. Please understand that we're not upset with you… we are getting upset because our thoughts are getting away from us. Our brain is a sieve and the thoughts are water… So… We get frustrated. After that, it keeps going… We expect the NTs around us to be able to tell that we are upset… I mean that is what they have going for them, isn't it? They have the super power of instant on empathy and the ability to read microexpressions…

Once we're upset, it goes downhill from there… The NTs keep interrupting and not seeing how upset we are, and we can't get our thoughts out… they are slipping away… and the dissonance creeps in… so we get snippy… JUST SO WE CAN SAY WHAT WE HAVE ORGANIZED IN OUR HEAD… So we blow up… and yell it…

I have actually been very rude to my friends, my long time partner, and other people… to the point of saying "Can you just shut the >>>Expletive redacted<<< up for a moment and let me talk? I have tried to say this same sentence for the last 5 minutes!"

When this happens, we are not trying to be rude… we are trying to rectify an internal conflict before it becomes a dissonant event and ruins our day… or even our week.

As usual, my admonition is to show patience… help us learn to realize when we are interrupting… and try to be understanding when we do it…

50 – I have Asperger's… Now What?

So… I have dedicated a lot of words in this blog to the importance of getting an official diagnosis when dealing with… Well… I've focused on Asperger's and Autism, but really… It is important to get a diagnosis for ANY mental health issue… but that is not what I need discuss to today…

You finally listened… to me, to someone else, to the discovery channel… You swallowed it down and went and got your diagnosis. You are officially an Autist or an Aspie. You've got your "this awkward moment brought to you by" card…

So… Now… what do you do? How do you move forward…

Let's start with one of the most important steps… ACCEPTANCE…

Normally, the word acceptance refers to others attitudes towards Autists… In this case, I am referring to the acceptance an Autist needs for himself. We have to accept ourselves… Not in the traditional way. We don't need to accept our condition… We need to accept that there is something wrong with us… we need to accept the fact that we may need cognitive behavioral therapy, socialization, accommodations or additional social skill training.

It seems like a no brainer, but this is a major step. A diagnosis means that it got real. It means that we have been told that we have a life effecting condition that will never go away. It can be a lot to take in. What's worse, is that most of are raised in an environment of understanding and care… which means that we are raised from an early age to believe that there is really nothing wrong with us… While a healthy dose of self esteem is important to mental and emotional health, it is makes it a lot more difficult to accept that we need to take the steps to help ourselves.

As much as it hurts (and believe me, I know how much it hurts, I've been there), you need to accept that there is (in spite of parental faith and love), indeed, something wrong with us.

Honestly, the next step is to find a specialist.

I hate to disparage people, but there are a lot of Psychologists that will argue with my next statement. You need a specialist. Most Psychs will say that they are equipped to handle an Aspie or an Autist, but they are wrong.

"Why is that, Feral One?"

Well… It's like this. Your average psychologist has read a few articles on the conditions… That's all the research they have done into our conditions… Well, that and the diagnostic criteria. That's it… So… your psychologist is going to know that you need some skill training, maybe some medication and cognitive behavioral therapy… but that is it… they will not be able to come up with an effective treatment plan. Most suffer from pride, and will tell you that they are equipped to deal with it, but this is patently false in most situations.

By contrast, your specialist will have a good grasp on the issues associated with Asperger's and Autism. There is a huge difference between knowing that Aspies have a tendency towards sensory issues and understanding the impact that sensory issues can have on an individual. Further, they will have dedicated a lot of time to understanding the condition, possible treatment programs, medications… AND they will be current on the research into Asperger's and Autism.

Next… and this is the big one… Take the treatment program suggested by your specialist… and take it to heart. I know this seems like a given, but it isn't… You really NEED to take what they have to say and RUN WITH IT. If they say you are need to try a medication, do it… Don't read the side effects – because you'll just give yourself a case of psychosomatic reactions… If they say you need to practice a specific cognitive technique, or a social skill… Step out of your damn comfort zone and just DO IT!

Embrace it. You've accepted that you needed a diagnosis. You've already accepted that you need help with some of these problems. You've spent the time and effort to find a specialist. TAKE THE ADVICE GIVEN YOU.

It's not easy. It's damn hard… I know… I've been in the thick of it. I've had to war with my own pride and brain to get to where I could improve as a human being. But let me tell you… It was totally worth it.

51 – I have a diagnosis… and now the world seems to be filled with Autistics

First off, I would like to thank FNORD from www.wrongplanet.net for this topic. I started a thread on the website and asked people to offer up ideas for topics for the series… I have gotten a couple great suggestions.

So… You've gone through all the steps… You've started with the self assessment tests… You've talked to your friends and family… and gone to a mental health professional… NOW – you have a diagnosis. An official diagnosis…

I've talked about where to go from here… I've talked about the pitfalls of excessive self esteem and denial of the basics of Autistic spectrum disorders… I've talked about Aspie/NT relations and some of the mechanisms that run in the background of the Aspie psyche… And I've talked about co-morbid conditions…

What I have only touched on is the the way some of the traits of Autistic spectrum disorders interact.

Human beings are, at their core, pattern seeking machines… This is why we see images in clouds and pictures in the stars… It is why we see the Virgin Mary in our toast and Jesus in our soup. In a Scientific American article (located HERE), researchers crafted studies to test human pattern seeking and recognition in college students… through 6 studies, the results were consistent…

"One experiment mimicked the stock market, while another asked students to search for images in television static. Time and again, students saw images where there were none and found stock patterns that didn't exist."

These experiments show that, on a basic level, the human

mind is a pattern seeking machine. Autists and Aspies, (as much as some of us hate to admit it) are human… The way we process input in a different way than NTs. Studies have shown that Autistic Spectrum Individuals have a higher level of attention to detail than most NTs. Add to that, the tendency of Aspies to hyperfocus and obsess over things that affect them personally… and we can draw some interesting conclusions…

As much as I am opposed to the DSM-V… the diagnostic criteria for an Autistic Spectrum Disorder is as follows:

I.   Persistent deficits in social communication and social interaction across multiple contexts, as manifested by the following, currently or by history (examples are illustrative, not exhaustive, see text):

    a) Deficits in social-emotional reciprocity, ranging, for example, from abnormal social approach and failure of normal back-and-forth conversation; to reduced sharing of interests, emotions, or affect; to failure to initiate or respond to social interactions.

    b) Deficits in nonverbal communicative behaviors used for social interaction, ranging, for example, from poorly integrated verbal and nonverbal communication; to abnormalities in eye contact and body language or deficits in understanding and use of gestures; to a total lack of facial expressions and nonverbal communication.

    c) Deficits in developing, maintaining, and understanding relationships, ranging, for example, from difficulties adjusting behavior to suit various social contexts; to difficulties in sharing imaginative play or in making friends; to absence of interest in peers.

II. Restricted, repetitive patterns of behavior, interests, or activities, as manifested by at least two of the following, currently or by history (examples are illustrative, not exhaustive; see text):

a) Stereotyped or repetitive motor movements, use of objects, or speech (e.g., simple motor stereotypes, lining up toys or flipping objects, echolalia, idiosyncratic phrases).

b) Insistence on sameness, inflexible adherence to routines, or ritualized patterns or verbal nonverbal behavior (e.g., extreme distress at small changes, difficulties with transitions, rigid thinking patterns, greeting rituals, need to take same route or eat food every day).

c) Highly restricted, fixated interests that are abnormal in intensity or focus (e.g, strong attachment to or preoccupation with unusual objects, excessively circumscribed or perseverative interest).Hyper- or hyporeactivity to sensory input or unusual interests in sensory aspects of the environment (e.g., apparent indifference to pain/temperature, adverse response to specific sounds or textures, excessive smelling or touching of objects, visual fascination with lights or movement).

III. Symptoms must be present in the early developmental period (but may not become fully manifest until social demands exceed limited capacities, or may be masked by learned strategies in later life).

IV. Symptoms cause clinically significant impairment in social, occupational, or other important areas of current functioning.

V. These disturbances are not better explained by intellectual disability (intellectual developmental disorder) or global developmental delay. Intellectual disability and autism spectrum disorder frequently co-occur; to make comorbid diagnoses of autism spectrum disorder and intellectual disability, social communication should be below that expected for general developmental level.

I have started writing this paragraph over and over again for well over an hour… I cannot find the specific wording that would be both accurate and politically correct… or even nice… So… Brutal honesty time…

I will break it down for you. Everyone has some of these traits. EVERYONE has some of these at times… especially in times of stress. This fact is the source of one of my least favorite sayings ever… "Isn't everyone just a little autistic?"

So… since Autists and Aspies take the pattern seeking thing to the extreme – we are going to notice this stuff a lot more than anyone else…

The main issue is that we are hyper-focused, hyper-vigilant (a trait often noted in Autists, and definitely in those with a co-morbid diagnosis of bipolar disorder), possessed of obsessive tendencies… All of these things lead to noticing the earmarks of Autism in others… Even if they are extremely NT…

What's worse is, for most of us, that we have been lonely our entire lives, and it is a relief to see that there is a reason for all of the oddities that make up the Autistic/Aspie personality. There is a sudden feeling that we belong to something, no matter how odd that group might be…

So, we are hoping against hope to find others. This leads us to search for others… Sometimes, we don't even know why we are searching… or even that we are…

What's worse… Is that this pattern seeking just happens. It's a basic function of the human brain and we do it all the time… We will try to find that diagnosis everywhere… Cartoon characters, TV characters, actors or actresses, sitcom characters, scientists and dead people… None of them are safe…

If you're an NT and you are "classified" as an Aspie by one of your friends or relatives… Take it for what it is… a compliment… we want you to belong to our circle…

I have touched on this topic in several issues of this blog before, but it has never been the focus of an issue… so… I think it deserves some extra time.

Being and Aspie or Autist is something that most NTs cannot wrap their heads around. This is not a lack of intelligence or empathy on their part. Neurotypicals are capable and intelligent… but Autism is so outside their ken that it is difficult for them to identify with us. A lot of Autists and Aspies lament this fact, but let's put this into perspective…

As an Aspie, I am often bewildered by the behaviors and reasoning of NTs. Their emotional responses, reasoning, instinctual responses, and logic abilities are a complete mystery to most Autistic Spectrum Individuals. What most Autists and Aspies do not understand is that we are as much a mystery to them as they are to us. That's right… They can't fathom our reasoning, logic, intellect and emotional responses any more than we can theirs…

Honestly… We can't see them in ourselves… I am in a unique position. As a film maker, I see myself on tape a lot. I also record a vlog… so I see my emotional responses a lot more than most Aspies. Let me tell you… We are… Hard to read at the best of times… The word that best describes us is "inscrutable".

I know this sounds odd, but trust me… it's true… what we think is showing clearly on our faces is not.

Watch this video if you don't believe me…
https://youtu.be/CQkwA2vi_Zc

At around the 5 minute mark… When I am showing the

rubble of the factory, I am almost in tears. My throat aches, my eyes are burning, and my voice is about to hitch… Literally, I felt like I was about to have an extreme and humiliating crying jag. (Please note that I kept the camera rolling in spite of that… I am that committed). But… it doesn't show. I KNOW that it is happening and I can't even see it on the video…

So, it is little wonder that we have a disconnect between us and the NTs around us.

The disconnect would not be an issue, except for the fact that we are all primates… Primates are social animals, and as such, there are instinctual reactions to behaviors outside of the mean for the social grouping. The effect is less evident with Aspies and Autistics, because we are often the one who is outside of the behavioral norm.

On the flip-side, I frequent a couple message boards dedicated to the Autistic condition. There are large groups of Aspies and Autistics on these boards. When it is just Autistic Spectrum individuals, the primate behaviors abound. The odd man out is often shunned or treated badly, just like Autistic Spectrum Individuals deal with when confronted by a group of NTs.

While growing up, this can be devastating to the self-esteem of Autistics.

The problem with this is that, to be able to benefit from the possible treatment options available to Autistic Spectrum Individuals, one must be able to function on a healthy emotional plane. being down on one's self can be the biggest stumbling block to advancement.

Parents of Autistic Spectrum Individuals want the best for their children… Well… Parents of NT children want the same for their children as well… but the parents of Autistic Spectrum Individuals have a long roe to hoe in front of them…

They will often end up overcompensating. As opposed to being completely honest with their children, they opt on the side of excessive caution.

This is something I don't understand. Autistics and Aspies tend to be grounded in fact… So much so, that a need for truth in our personal reality can interfere with those social relationships we so desperately crave.

So… because the parents worry about their children so very much, they will speak platitudes… "There's nothing wrong with you." – "You're just wired differently." – "People just need to accept you for what you are… a special snowflake."

While these concepts are important for a healthy self-esteem and the possibility of treatment and social skills training… They are hazardous to the Autistic Spectrum Individual. When I say hazardous, I am not talking to one's physical health – instead, I am talking about their possibility for normalization and socialization.

Think about this… Most treatments involve the practices of cognitive behavioral therapy and skill training.

"Skill Training?" You ask?

Yes, skill training… the behaviors of social groups are dictated by social skills… They are called skills because they are just that… They are skills… skills can be learned…

Now comes the part that will be difficult for most NTs that have an Autistic Spectrum Individual in your life… Believe it or not… Most of us NEED the cognitive behavioral therapy and social skill training… BUT…

And this is a big but…

If we believe that there is nothing wrong with us… If we have the self esteem required to be comfortable with ourselves, then we are not capable of the mindset required to benefit from any possible training, therapy or help.

Ironically enough… If we have excessive self esteem, it gets worse… Since we feel that there is nothing wrong with us… We will believe (possibly rightly, possibly wrongly) that the rest of the world is filled with irrational, illogical, loud, nosy and overly emotional people… That is to say, NTs… but since there is nothing wrong with us, it must be something wrong with the rest of the world. We will believe that the inability of the rest of the world to engage in hyperfocus means that we are surrounded by mental defectives… The fact that the rest of the world does not engage in special interests and obsessive tendencies means that we are surrounded by lazy and unmotivated people…

In short – if we have excessive self-esteem, we are arrogant asshats…

I know… the wording of this issue is combative and a bit snarky… but I speak from experience… I was one of those snotty, arrogant asshats… I really was…

I spent years after my diagnosis… in DENIAL… There was nothing wrong with me… It was all of you that were flawed… I was an ass… plain and simple… And since I was certain there was nothing wrong with me… I avoided the mental health professionals… they just wanted money from me… I fought the diagnosis, training and therapy… In short… I was insufferable… And it was because I was told that there was nothing wrong with me… I believed it… I believed it to the very center of my being…

We walk a fine line between the special needs of our condition and the needs of our personality and soul… Be careful before you tell your Autistic Spectrum Child that there is NOTHING wrong with them… this can be devastating later in life… hell… it can make their lives miserable now…

These days, we hear the phrase "Self-advocacy" thrown a lot. But what, exactly, is self advocacy?The dictionary defines an advocate as *"a person who speaks or writes in support or defense of a person, cause, etc."*

It goes on to define advocacy as *"the act of pleading for, supporting, or recommending; active espousal:"*

So… at the root of it all, an advocate will practice advocacy… I know that is a given, but it really is necessary to explain. And advocate is one who takes up a concept and crusades for it. They plead the case, make noise and help people become aware of the concept.

I know you've heard about advocacy groups… Some well known ones are the ASPCA, PETA, The ACLU, The Audubon Society… And finally… you cannot have a discussion about advocacy and Autism without mentioning Autism Speaks… All of these groups are advocates for their causes… and they do a damn good job at it. (The previous statement is, in no way, an endorsement of Autism Speaks)

I am a firm believer in advocacy… Some people need someone to step up and speak for them… However, I believe that a successful advocate needs to have a frame of reference… be able to understand the person that they are speaking for… And that, I honestly believe, is not really possible with Autistic Spectrum Disorders.

I have spent the last year writing this series -"Care and Feeding of Your Aspie" for just that reason… To help Neurotypicals develop at lease a modicum of understanding of what it means to be an Autistic Spectrum Individual. We spend our lives looking through the Warped Lens of Our Own

Perceptions. We experience the world through a miswired brain… and we don't have the frame of reference to even express the differences… Honestly… for every issue in the Care and Feeding series, there are hours of research… And then are hours of discussion with my pet Neurotypicals to hammer out examples and reference points…

To give you and idea of what I am talking about, I will refer you to several previous entries. (Sorry about being self referential, but I believe these entries help put things in perspective)
- Sensory Issues
- Aspies, Pain and Perception
- Food Issues
- Cognitive Dissonance, Decision Making and Communication

At it's core… the entire series is about autistic perceptions, but this specific entries personify these issues more so than others…

We have established that Autistic perceptions and cognitive processes are different than Neurotypicals; and that an advocate needs to truly understand that which they are speaking for; and without extensive explanation and education, it is almost impossible for an NT to comprehend the Autistic condition… SO… Ask yourself… are they qualified to be your advocate?

The answer, in most cases, is (or should be) a resounding NO.

So… You are an Autistic Spectrum Individual… you need an advocate, but no one else has the frame of reference to successfully speak for you… Who should it be?

And that, right there, is the point of self-advocacy… No one else can truly speak for you… Autistic perceptions pretty much guarantee that.

Now, I know the next question… "How do I act a self-advocate?"

Believe it or not… That is simple…

Speak for yourself… Educate those around you. Blog about it… When you hear people say ignorant things about Autistic Spectrum Disorders, see it as an education opportunity. Tell everyone… declare proudly, "I am Autistic and proud of it."

It's a difficult step to take… Speaking from experience… Telling a health care professional (that was not my Mental Health care professional) that I was a "Special Needs Adult" was one of the hardest steps I have ever taken… But once I got past that, it became easier.

Take that first step… and speak for yourself…

Oh… on a personal note… this is not encouragement to be an ass… as with all things, I always espouse a personal ethos of respectful behavior… even to those you don't agree with… ESPECIALLY with those people.

54 – You aren't Autistic… You HAVE autism.

I was speaking to a woman recently. I told her that I was
Autistic. She sucked her teeth at me and said, with an air of
authority (and i quote) – *"You aren't Autistic… You HAVE
autism."* First of all… Screw you… I'm the autistic… I have the
right to label myself as such. And secondly – I really do hate the
politically correct movement.

And that is what her statement is… *"You aren't Autistic… You
HAVE autism."* is a way of saying that I am not defined by my
disease… And I see why this would be important to a
neurotypical. However, words are important… labels exist to
allow us to understand the world in a way that our brains can
relate to. We need labels so that we can communicate in a
meaningful way with those around us. When I say cup, or plate
– because of the framework of labels we have worked out in
advance, you have an idea of what I am talking about…

And that is what being Autistic really is… When
communicating with other people (NT's and Autists alike), the
word conveys an idea… And since there are as many forms of
Autism as there are Autistics +1 (one form every Autistic and
the +1 is for the DSM version.), LITERALLY – all we can do is
convey the basic concept of what it is to be Autistic. So… I
personally feel that the word Autistic is a valid and acceptable
label for me… and I will be damned if I will be told that I mean
something else when I speak.

The politically correct movement started out in sort of the
same thing… It was an Idea, not a movement. The whole
concept was respect.

Language is an important tool. Without language, we have
VERY limited ability to communicate… We can make general
groanings, grunts and growls. The problem is, language is an

imprecise, yet powerful tool. Words, to a certain extent, have power…

Think carefully about it… Racial slurs are but one example… These words have the power to hurt, enrage and minimize.

So, the concept of political correctness is one of respect… By choosing words and phrases (Like "African American", "Autistic Spectrum Individual", and the like), political correctness seeks to convey respect and stop the minimalization of the people being discussed.

It has done a lot of good, but it can hurt as well…

While the concept of political correctness is good… it has turned into something far more malicious…

Instead of trying to pay homage, convey respect and reduce minimalization… it has become a way to control. It controls the way we think. It controls the way we speak. And it controls the way we behave.

Think about it… Back in the day, Autistic Spectrum Individuals were routinely referred to as "Retards". By following the concepts of political correctness, it evolved to the point that we are now called Autistic Spectrum Individuals… This stopped the minimalization of my people in one way… but it continued it in a couple other ways…

When we were called "retards," anyone who heard about it, knew what to expect… even though it was (more often than not) wrong… Now that we have been granted the label of "Autistic Spectrum Individual", we have another label to live with…

Now, we are faced with the label of Autism. Think about all of the things I write about… This is part 54 of the series… That is 53 other issues designed to combat the preconceived notions about Autistic Spectrum Disorders. We are labeled Autistic Spectrum Individuals… And with that label, comes it's own minimalization. The average person has a mold that they pour us into when they hear the term…

While I agree, in concept, with Political Correctness… However, I disagree when it impacts me directly. I disagree when people tell me how to talk about myself… I am opposed to people being told that they cannot choose their own labels…

So…I am autistic… like it or lump it.

55 – You think YOUR teen years were hard.

When most people think back to their teenage years, they remember a time of tempestuous emotion, hormone changes, and other difficulties… I will say that I try not to minimize anyone's personal experiences, but this is one time that I really have no choice…

The changes of puberty are already a nightmare… Hormones – the body is making a transition from our child form to a sexually mature creature. This comes with pain (both and physical and emotional), hormones, and changes in brain chemistry. Cognitive abilities – the modes of thought that got us through childhood are no longer useful (we no longer need to be an information sponge to survive, and are developing a cognitive model that will allow us to reason and survive as an adult of the species)… Social understanding – we move from info sponge to social creature… a necessary step for the social creature that humans are.

Add these things to the difficulties of Asperger's and Autism and you have a perfect storm… And here are just some of the reasons why.

Since we've been talking about hormones… Let's… ummm… keep talking about them…Since most Autistic Spectrum individuals are isolated by the social issues that accompany the condition, we don't have even the knowledge passed on by our peers… Yes, it is uninformative, and outright wrong in many cases, but we don't even have that. This leaves us clueless about sex – which can lead to awkward moments, excruciating social situations and horrible sexual encounters later in life. Aspie boys can end up obsessed with porn and masturbation. Aspie girls can make advances and give sexual cues that she does not understand.

We are not able to truly be a teenager. This is a generalization, but teens are concerned with fashions, styles, and fads. There is a lot of peer pressure to commit, submit and participate in these ritualistic displays of conformity. We are not able to do this. With sensory issues, clothing must be comfortable… And with the tendency of fashion to be less than comfortable, we can't do it… And even if we DO have the right clothing, it is unlikely that we will wear it in the proper manner and will always be about 15 degrees off cool… at least at this point in our life. Once we find hairstyles that work for us, we are unlikely to change it… even with the currents of fashion. Further, boys will often forget to shave; both boys and girls will often forget to comb their hair.

Hans Asperger described Aspies as "little professors." As a result, even from a young age, we come across as little adults. We can be rule-oriented, knowledgeable far above our age range, and a bit stiff. The teenage world is full of pitfalls… Any mis-step can lead to the teenager being ostracized… We have odd mannerisms – loud, avoid eye contact, interrupt in conversation, has no concept of personal space, and steer the conversation in the direction of our interests, willful, selfish, aloof… As a result, we are isolated and alone… after years of this, we are too anxious to initiate social contact… so it continues.

Often, we fall behind in our interests, clothes and hobbies. I am almost 40, and I collect toys. Another Aspie I know is into my little pony and classic cartoons. While we have other interests, getting out of them and moving into dating can be difficult.

We have problems with organization. While most of us can make it through elementary school easily… The lack of organization skills make high school ridiculously hard… It was difficult in one class… Now we have 6, six different teachers…

And I can assure you (and this is from personal experience) at lease one of those teachers is going to be uncooperative or outright oppositional to the concept of special accommodations for students… This can lead to failures at school, and that attracts attention to the student which makes them uncomfortable and that just makes it worse.

Aspies, in a desperate attempt to fit in can fall into the wrong crowds, simply because these people will accept them. This can lead to issues with sex and drugs which can then lead to encounters with the police… these don't go well. The Aspie tendency towards frankness and honesty can get them in trouble. Often, the police will interpret excessive honesty as being smart-ass.

I know… this is rambling and disjointed… and not at all inclusive or complete… but these were the issues that I had. I hope that these examples help you when preparing your Autistic Spectrum Individual.

56 – Why Does He Have to Talk? – or – Nonverbal Events

I often pull inspiration for issues of this series from several sites that I belong to. This one comes from www.wrongplanet.net.

A man is concerned about his son. The boy is 15 and lives with his mother in another state. The boy, recently has stopped talking to everyone but his father. He won't speak to his teachers, classmates, friends or mother. He has asked the community how to help the boy communicate with others.

This seems like a simple situation, but it is more complex than the imagery would imply.

Let's start with the different types of non-verbal behavior…

The first kind is what I engage in on many occasions. I don't have anything to say. Since the Aspie brain is a thing of stark contrast with little middle ground, we have to be engaged to want to communicate. In a world filled with NTs, it is rare that we are engaged. NTs are able to talk… often about nothing (That is, honestly, what small talk is). Most of the time, we don't speak when there is nothing to say. Small talk eludes us, because it rarely has a point.

Let me reword this. The social construct of small talk has a point. It is a form of bonding. It tests the neural and psychological compatibility of those we are surrounding ourselves with by eliciting responses that fall within a specific data set that declares that the person the NT is talking to is the kind of person that we like to spend time with. This specific social behavior is outside the ken of most Autistic Spectrum Individuals. Small talk doesn't impart any information of any import, and that, is (at least in the Autists mind) the point of communication.

As such… small talk isn't something we can do.

The second kind is what I refer to as dissonant silence. I am pretty sure that there is a word for it in psychological terminology, but I am not now (nor have I ever been and probably never will be) a mental health professional.

I have discussed the Autistic/Aspie decision making process as it pertains to cognitive dissonance.

When faced with social situations, it can be difficult for your Aspie. Often, we have learned some new social skill, had something explained to us, or picked up a new conversational gambit and will try it out. We go in with confidence… and then it fails, falling flat in a way that is debilitating. You see, it may be arrogant, but because of obsessive tendencies and special interests, we are used to being an expert in almost anything we engage in. We learn all there is to know about it…

And then there is the dreaded social situation. We are unable to work those things out. We can't… It seems to us that social situations are a bit like global weather patterns… If we could fathom all of the variables in this insanely complex mathematical system, we could figure it all out… but, like the weather, there are just way too many variables to pull it off. Since we can't do the math correctly, it is humiliating.

Since we are not used to being out of our depth… we are confronted by our own inadequacy… And THAT causes dissonance. We try to solve the math problem and fail. And as a self defense mechanism (to prevent psychological damage from continued dissonance), we will often stop talking in most social situations. If we don't say anything, we cannot be perceived as autistic, or weird…

Eventually, we will work our way out of it… as long as people aren't pushing… pushing reinforces the fact that our behavior in this instance is not normal, which can cause further dissonance.

The last type of nonverbal behavior is the one that is problematic. Nonverbal incidents can be a result of any number of things… over-stimulation, social pressure, anxiety, fear, pain… Simply put, something has caused an over stimulation of neural processes (not to be confused with sensory over-stimulation). The normal functioning of the brain is suspended during this event.

Often, these non-verbal events will be accompanied by stimming, repetitive motions, non-communicative verbalizations, pacing, rapid blinking, any combination of the above or something completely unique to your Autist that indicates an aberrant neural event.

In these situations, your Autist needs help…
I covered this in depth in a couple different issues. I will not cover the same information in depth, but this is a quick run down.
1. Safety First – do not restrain, be safe.
2. Communicate – since they are non-verbal let them know you are taking care of them.
3. Attempt to rectify the situation – post haste – Remove the stimulus or remove the autist from the situation.
4. Limit Stimuli – Take your Autist to a safe location that is quiet and not too bright.
5. Physically calm your Aspie – Some autists respond well to massage therapy.
6. Help Them – Help them be comfortable and help them in the situation.
7. Speak in Soothing Tones – A simple soothing tone can

help calm your Autist a great deal.

8. Stay Calm – not being calm can really exacerbate the situation.

9. Sometimes, it will happen – you can do all the right things and a tantrum, event or meltdown will still happen. This is not a reflection on you in any way.

This entry was prompted by a discussion on Wrong Planet. It is a clarification of points made in a discussion about perceived violence from Autistic Spectrum Individuals… I am not going to be discussing the original topic, but instead focusing on my opinion of Point of View.

I believe that there i a fundamental disconnect between Autistic Spectrum Individuals and Neurotypicals. I have already upset some people with my beliefs on why this is so, but I believe that it is an accurate assessment.

Autistic Spectrum Individuals live in a bit of a vacuum. We exist in a world run by NTs. The reasons for this are manifold, but boil down to a few small things.

1. There are a lot more of them than there are of us. According to the current numbers, 1.13% of the population are on the spectrum. I believe this number is a LOT lower due to over diagnosis.
2. Due to an inability to function in open (due to sensory issues, NT social rituals, and the oddity of NT interaction), we tend to stay in the wings.
3. Due to the stigma attached to mental illness (If it is in the DSM, by definition it is an mental illness), many family members are ashamed, and we end up ashamed of ourselves and hiding.
4. Public perception of Autistic Spectrum Individuals is flawed due to the myths perpetuated by outdated diagnostics, old books that should never have been printed, a misunderstanding of science, and continued flawed media representation.

In recent days, the media has been firing warning shots up our noses instead of across them. There have been a couple mass shootings in the last two years that have been attributed by mass media to individuals with Asperger's Syndrome. I can recall 4 of them… In only one instance was this the case. As a result, there is a firestorm of media attention… Negative attention. They are stating that Autistic Spectrum Individuals are prone to violence. NTs, not knowing better, believe it.

I can't blame them, really. In the last 50 years, we have gone from our only sources of information were books, periodicals and experts to the internet. We had to find books on the subject, or talk to the experts to get any information… That made information precious. It meant that to learn something, we actually had to work for it. Now, with the internet, the whole of human experience and knowledge is available to us at our fingertips. We are exposed to so much information that it is almost impossible, without a relatively new skill (internet research and distillation of misinformation) to know what is accurate and what is not.

So, the NTs see (hear, read, are told) a story about several Aspies who went on shooting sprees. They take a moment to do some research into Autistic Spectrum Disorders and find articles about sensory overloads, stimming, tantrums and meltdowns. They read that, during times of duress and great stress, they find that there may be *violent* outbursts.

We come to another aspect of the NT condition. Most of them don't really KNOW the definitions of the words they use. The way NTs learn is almost completely context sensitive. Context sensitive learning means that they have an idea of what it means because they were able to glean it from surrounding words… Most of them don't bother to look up the words to make sure… So… They read violent outbursts and the definition that pops into their head is this:
"caused by injurious or destructive force: a violent death."

When in reality, violent outbursts refers to the following

definition:
"intense in force, effect, etc.; severe; extreme."

And here is where the disconnect begins. NTs learn through this process. I don't have a name for it, but let's just call it Context Understanding. Everything is context sensitive. Words take on emotional connotations due to context they are used in. This is true for all things in the NT world, social situations, words, writing, communication… it's all context sensitive.

One of the biggest problems that Autistic Spectrum Individuals (especially Aspies) face is the fact that we tend to view things as absolute. We tend to deal in black and white, which interferes in understanding the context sensitive world. So, while the Autist understands that violent outbursts simply means that they are intense outbursts, not destructive – the NT, not having read the definitions, is limited to the context they learned the word violent in.

All of that was written to give you a framework to understand the next point – NTs, without it being explained to them, have no context for Autistic Perceptions. Since they make up 98.87% of the population, chances are, most NTs have never met an Autistic Spectrum Individual. If they have, our tendency to be relatively private about our condition (due to negative reactions from the context sensitive world), they did not realize it.

Because everyone else (98.87%) that they encounter learns the same way they do, share the basic machinery of perception and reason that they do, they assume that everyone thinks the same way. While this is not true, since they have not encountered it in someone else, they have no context for it.

That 1.13% that has an Autistic Spectrum Disorder is in the same boat. We are not part of the context sensitive world, AND really don't comprehend it. Just as NTs don't understand the methods for cognition, learning and emotional processing in themselves, Autists are rarely aware of the mechanisms in their own heads.

Now… Autists see the NTs accept each other out of hand. This is because the NTs are the standard. They accept each other without question (or minimal questioning) in most cases because they are all working on a basis of the context sensitive world and as a result, they present the proper signals for each other to cue in on. The Autists want to be able to be accepted the same way. Because of the mechanisms behind Autistic cognition, we don't give the signals. Therefore, the NT is made exceptionally uneasy. This is on them, but it is something that they cannot help. This is the way they are wired.

NTs are capable of adaptation in a very real and terrifying (terrifying because we are completely unable to do it) way, due to the context sensitive nature of their emotional and intellectual functioning. But since they have never encountered us before, they have no idea what they are dealing with. Since they can't read us, they get nervous. Simply put (and I have more than one NT that has explained this to me), those that cannot be read easily are one of the following:
1. Deceiving – obfuscating their signals in such a way to hide their intent.
2. Mentally Ill – "It's the quiet ones you have to watch out for" really sums this up.
3. Another species – when dealing with dogs and cats, you have to learn a completely new series of body language.

In essence, since we don't send the signals they expect, we come across as entirely alien. There is a concept called the uncanny valley.

"The uncanny valley is a hypothesis in the field of human aesthetics which holds that when human features look and

move almost, but not exactly, like natural human beings, it causes a response of revulsion among human observers. Examples can be found in the fields of robotics, 3D computer animation, and in medical fields such as burn reconstruction, infectious diseases, neurological conditions, and plastic surgery. The "valley" refers to the dip in a graph of the comfort level of humans as subjects move toward a healthy, natural human likeness described in a function of a subject's aesthetic acceptability."

So, here we are, on an instinctual level, make them uneasy.

Since those around us, educators, family members and our friends tend to accept us without question, we have come to expect it. We tend to have a small contingent of close friends… this means that we have people that accept us around us all of the time. We become accustomed to it. So, when we encounter new NTs, we expect the same thing from them as well… but we don't get it.

At this point, I have used the word "arrogance" to describe our behavior.
"characterized by or proceeding from arrogance, or a sense of superiority, self-importance, or entitlement"

We assume that we deserve acceptance from the outset… We assume that NTs should get it. We assume that they think the same way we do… Ironically enough, NTs make the same assumptions. The problem is that everyone on the planet is restricted to their own Point of View. We are limited to the view through the warped lens of our own experiences and perceptions.

While other Autists will get it (for the most part) because we share the same mechanisms for cognition and behavior, NTs will not.

The reason I use the word arrogant is because we will expect instant acceptance from NTs and expect them to understand something outside of their context sensitive world… This is something that takes a lot of work to explain to them… It takes a LOT of work to make them understand (as evinced by the fact that this is part 57 of this series). The reason that it is arrogant is because we will talk about it and try to make them understand… but for the most part, a majority of Autists and Aspies will NOT take the time to try to understand NT cognition or reasoning mechanisms.

On the whole, we Autists will expect acceptance, but do not give the same level of acceptance to the NTs we know. We expect them to make accommodations for us, but are not willing to do the same… Or worse, do not even see the need for it. This sense of entitlement makes us arrogant… in fact and in perception. As I have said before, perception is everything.

A friend of mine on Wrong Planet brought up the following response to these very points.

"I can't drive. Why? Because I'm overloaded with stimuli when I do, there are too many variables to account for and all of them have to be observed all the time. Normal people can do that because they're able to process that information, I can't so it would be dangerous (and highly irresponsible) for me to drive, not only for myself, but others as well. Would it be arrogant then, to ask for a ride from people without that issue?"

My response to this – that is the opposite of arrogance, because this is ASKING for assistance… NOT expecting it.

So… how do we, as a community and individuals, defeat this arrogance (either in fact or perception)? By remembering the following: The NTs we deal with in more than a passion manner are as bewildered and flummoxed as we are by our interactions. They need to know that we are all in the same boat. Tell them that you are an Autist… Explain your particular form of Autistic Perception and how it effects them… give them time to adjust… Do not EXPECT them to just get it. On the flip side, it is arrogant to only talk about our perceptions… And they will feel that way… SO… Listen to their NT perceptions, ask questions, try to understand them… and what's more… TRY to accommodate them.

Remember… if they are your friend or attempting to interact with you, they are already making an effort. They are trying to accommodate you. So, return the favor.

If it is someone who does not want to, does not care that you are an Autist, they aren't worth your time anyway…

58 – My Tummy Hurts.

There have been several studies in recent years that have revealed something interesting. According to these studies, more than 50% of Autistic Spectrum Individuals suffer from gastro-intestinal problems. Often there will be digestive problems, food allergies and the like. There has been a lot of discussion about these issues, but there is no one answer for keeping these issues under control…

In 43% of Autistic Spectrum Individuals these studies found an "altered intestinal permeamility" that was not found in the Neurotypicals that were also in the study. This means that there are spaces in the intestinal tract of these Autists that do not exist in the NTs studied. This altered permeability allows microscopic particles of ingested materials to enter the blood stream. This triggers an incorrect Immunoglobulin A response in the body.

What this means is that something really technical happens that I don't completely understand… or rather, I understand it, but not well enough to explain it to someone else… Simply put, Immunoglobulin A is part of an immune response that is important for mucus membrane health… The entire gastro-intestinal system is a mucus membrane.

Since the foods are not processed properly, the body views these particles as microbial invaders… When these invaders are detected, Immunoglobulin A (an antibody) is dispatched to the site. It deals with these errant particles and all is well… However (like with other immune responses), future responses will be more severe. When these specific particles are encountered again, the release of antibodies results in an inflammatory response in the gut. If this inflammation continues and becomes chronic, it causes the Immunoglobulin A levels in the gut to fall. This can lead to an increase in intestinal fauna which can cause more problems.

The gut is a finely balanced ecosystem, and any imbalance can be an issue. Some of the problems that can develop as a result of this are:

- an inhibition of b12 absorption – b12 is essential for metabolizing carbohydrates and fats. It is also necessary for the synthesis of proteins and the myelin sheaths on neurons.
- bacterial growth can destroy enzymes in the intestines that can further inhibit carbohydrate processing.
- Excessive microbial growth results in the fauna competing for nutrients and results in the bacterial wastes being deposited in the gut.
- Yeast can flourish, produce acid and damage the intestinal walls.

Add this stuff to the issues with stress that Autistic Spectrum Individuals tend to have and we have a a miserable person. Stress can contribute to stomach issues in the following ways:

- throat spasms
- stress can trigger "fight or flight" which can shut down digestion
- stress can cause further inflammation of gastro-intestinal tissues
- can cause over or under eating

All of this makes for an uncomfortable and miserable Autist. An uncomfortable and miserable Autist often has behavioral problems as a result. And the issue with this is that the behavioral problems can lead to further GI distress, which can exacerbate behavioral problems which can lead to more GI distress… I think you can see where this is going…

So… how do we deal with this?

First of all, I have always advocated finding the RIGHT doctor for your Autist. This is someone who will listen and consider what you have to say… If your Autist has gut problems, speak to your doctor about the possibility of testing for Intestinal Permeability and talk about possible Rx treatments to restore the balance of fauna in their gut.

There are alternative methods that are supposed to control this balance (specifically, carb control), but I warn against this because there are no studies on the subject that I can find.

Lastly… Reduce the stress in your Autists… If you do not know how to do that, I will be discussing that soon.

59 – I just don't like him.

This issue was inspired by personal experience… I went to a party for New Years Eve. I have scrubbed references to the location and the name of the event from this account. What I will reveal is that it was at a shop dedicated to one of my hobbies, and there were about 30 people there.

A couple hours before the new year, we started playing one of my favorite games… Cards Against Humanity. (http://www.cardsagainsthumanity.com/). Cards Against Humanity is a game for horrible people. The game is ridiculously simple. Players have a hand of white cards. A black card with a question is drawn, and all the players play white cards to answer it the question. The funniest (and often the most morally offensive, socially insensitive and just plain wrong) answers will win.

ANYWAY..

We were playing Cards Against Humanity (CAH) one of the friends of the owner of the store came in. INSTANTLY… I didn't like her. This happens from time to time… On more than one occasion, my NT friends have stated that I am over-reacting and that I should give everyone a chance. And to be fair, in the last 30 years… I have been wrong… twice… So… I do give these people a chance.

I will give them a REAL chance… And, honestly, on more than one occasion, I actually got to know a person and liked them, in spite of my initial reaction to them… HOWEVER… with the exception of those two people… Every one of these people has proven that my perceptions were right.

I suppose some explanation is really in order.

Since you have an Aspie in your life, I know you spend a lot of time being confused by their behavior (unless you are one of those awesome, and rare people who just gets us)… I know there has been at least one instance where you introduced your Aspie to someone and within 30 seconds, your Aspie made it clear that they didn't like the person that you just introduced them to. And I am not talking about just a "meh" reaction… I am talking full on dislikes them. (if you haven't encountered it before now, wait – you're young yet)…

I want to start out by saying that NTs, on the whole, are more accepting of others than Aspies. It is just a fact. If you go back and read the rest of the issues in this series, you will see why. As an Aspie develops mentally and emotionally, we learn what we like in ourselves and others, and are not very open to new experiences when it comes to people. Those experiences can be very traumatic… or worse – apocalyptic.

So, when we meet a new person, we automatically analyze everything about that person. Speech patterns, behavioral ticks, word choice, body language. This analysis takes just a moment. Once the information is gathered it is compared against the templates of people that we know we like. There is an acceptable margin of error, allowing us to incorporate new people into our circle of friends. But if someone that we have just met does not meet those templates, we aren't likely to like them straight off… but they may have a chance to become a friend.

We have also collated templates of those people that we actively dislike. If that person displays personality traits and behavior that match those template we will dislike them, or in some cases hate them… INSTANTLY…

I bring this up because that happened to me on New Years Eve.

Often, I advocate working with your Aspie to overcome what ever issue that I am discussing… but not this time. I don't have any advice on how to avoid this behavior.

What I can advise is this… Don't force it. Trying to make an Aspie like someone or something that they don't like will ONLY lead to problems… Oppositional behavior, hostility and acting out are very possible… and it can lead to dissonant episodes as the Aspie tries to rectify pretending to like someone against the reality of the situation.

The advice I can give is to acknowledge it. They don't like the person and they don't know why. Fine. Deal with it. We have our reasons, and most of the time, they are not wrong.

60 – Repetitive Behaviors and Meaningless Ritual

According to studies, Autistic Spectrum Individuals tend to engage in ritual behavior.

I have found many studies on the subject but the abstract on THIS ONE states it clearly and succinctly.
"Ritual behavior, while often considered as nonpurposeful or problematic, can also be regarded as functional behavior for individuals with autism spectrum disorders (ASD). This study investigated the types and characteristics of ritual behavior in children with ASD…"

So, there ya have it – ritual behaviors, wile problematic can be regarded as functional behavior. Excellent… We have a psychological behavior model that is justified and functional behavior… Now here's the question… What is ritual behavior.

From a psychological standpoint, ritual behavior is:
"a technical sense for a repetitive behavior systematically used by a person to neutralize or prevent anxiety; it is a symptom of obsessive–compulsive disorder."

There it is… Again, ritual is explained as a way for the brain to relieve anxiety.

Autistic Spectrum Disorders are often noted for having obsessive tendencies and interests. As you know, we often refer to these as "special interests." However, there is a lot more to it than that. It may not be a special interest, but instead something we need to do… and in some cases, it is just some thing we do.

What does this mean for you and your Autist?

It means that when we get stressed or experience anxiety (and this source can be from any source – those I have discussed previously or others.), we can engage in ritualistic behavior to alleviate this stress and anxiety.

Some examples:
Due to post traumatic disorder, my sister has debilitating nightmares. It makes getting any rest difficult, which adds to her stress levels and anxiety and will often result in a fear response as a part of her normal morning function. In the first 8 minutes after awaking, three things need to happen… she has to brush her teeth, get a cup of coffee, and do some rudimentary stretching (due to catastrophic injuries when we were young). It is not the caffeine in the coffee that she needs, it is the ritual of making the coffee. As she states – "There are more efficient ways to get caffeine; pills, energy drinks, or soda." Often, that cup of coffee is neglected after only a sip is taken. If this ritual is not observed, her mental equilibrium is shot for the entire day.

My sister and I both grew up in the city. As such, our brains developed with the sounds of the city and it is burned into the neural pathways permanently. When we lived in Arabi, LA – the sound levels were perfect… we were a block from the National Guard Base, 3 blocks from the river with river traffic, half a mile from the Domino Sugar Factory and 3 miles from several fuel refineries. The sound levels were perfect and the smell, while most people thought it was horrible… smelled like the city. It was perfect. Then… We moved to uptown New Orleans. It is a quiet neighborhood, little in the way of traffic or children (in spite of being a few blocks from a school). It is quiet… way too quiet… So, our house always has music, or a TV or the like going… just for background noise. To sleep, once we moved here, I need a white noise generator.

Netflix is constantly going, watching the same shows over and over – as part of the ritual. Scrubs, Stargate SG-1, Farscape, and Futurama… Constantly… even though we can quote them like Bill Murray in the movie: Groundhog Day.

It's annoying to our NT companions, but they are accustomed to it.

For me, when stressed… I play Diablo 3… I have beaten the game on all modes, gotten some awesome gear, and can play through it with my eyes closed. One of my roommates plays with me because he enjoys seeing how massively obscene the amount of destruction can be.

We do these things and they can be annoying to be around us when we do. But I haven't address why we do it.

Like with so many things, it is a way to relieve psychological pressure. When an NT encounters a situation that throws them off balance the cognitive dissonance mechanic within their brains counters it with distraction. Aspies and Autists do not seem to have this functionality to their Dissonance mechanic. I believe this has to do with the obsessive nature of Autistic Spectrum dissonance…

Since we lack the shades of gray in want, desire and dissonance, a dissonant event will just feedback… As such, we have to distract ourselves from it all… And that is where ritual comes in. Our rituals key into neural pathways that that have been etched into our brains… When confronted by a dissonant situation, we are able to switch modes by engaging in ritual. The dissonant even will take second fiddle once we engage in the ritual. Basically, we are forcing our minds to function along those burned in neural pathways… Since the brain knows how to handle the ritualistic behavior… the dissonance can be ignored and (in most cases) will fade as the subconscious mind processes the causes of the dissonant event.

So, while it may be annoying to you as the NT, it is necessary for your Aspie. I suggest getting into it… Hell, we can always use someone to play the Wizard in Diablo 3.

61 – I don't know what to call this essay

If you've read my blog, then you are probably aware of the fact that I am a photographer. I have been taking photos since I was six.

Now, this and of itself, has nothing to do with my condition… But the way my thought processes and perceptions have evolved were completely dependent on this lifelong obsession and interest.

Recently, my permanent partner and I were discussing my work and my obsession with it, and she brought up an interesting point. My camera(s) allow me to do something that I would not be able to do otherwise – I am able, when in public, to use the lens as a way to distance myself from what is going on around me.

Many Autistic Spectrum Individuals have sensory issues (which I discuss HERE) – myself included. And this makes it difficult to interact and survive in the outside world. When overwhelmed by sound, lights, sights and sensations, it can be difficult to do anything more than walk… Irritability, irrationality and anxiety can result.

Somehow, I have managed to cobble together a self defense mechanism based on my special interest.

The lens of my camera, since it views the world differently that my eyes do, allows me to take a step back from the situation. I have spent a lot of time working on learning to view the world and see what my camera will see. This has led to my being able to analyze the way light falls on an object, the way form and color make up the world and the way focus effects everything. In situations that aggravate my sensory issues, I can use my camera.

Part of it is the different way it allows me to see the world. Part of it is the fact that I can (almost literally) hide behind the view finder like it was a shield. Part of it is that, when you are wielding a camera, people will leave you alone. For some reason, the very presence of a lens acts like a force field… Most people don't want to get in front of a camera.

I think that has a lot to do with the fact that most people really don't really know how they look and seeing photos of themselves causes cognitive dissonance…

Anyway… The reason that I brought this up is that I believe this may be applicable to other Autistic Spectrum Individuals. After discussing with a couple of other Austists and Aspies, I have developed the theory that focus can help alleviate the issues in question.

Part of the reason we get overwhelmed so easily is that we process massive amounts of data in ways that most NTs do not. If you can find something that your Autist can focus on, it may take some of that processing power and divert it from sensory processing and into something less intrusive. I could be completely wrong about that, but I suspect that I'm not…

Try it and let me know?

62 – A bit more on special interests

I should write a great deal… Let me reword that… I should write more on THIS series.

But I can't.

Let me explain… Writing is one of my "Special Interests." As previously discussed, special interests are obsessive in nature and release hormones that create a sense of pleasure, satisfaction and well being in your Aspie. And writing is one of my LIFE-LONG interests… That means that it is a special interest that never faded. So… Simply put, I can't NOT write. I HAVE to write.

The problem is not with writing, but focusing on one thing TO write. To give you an idea – at this moment I have one play script, this series, two partly completed novels, the revisions on two other novels, and a couple film scripts I am working on. So, you can see, I am constantly writing.

The biggest problem I have with writing on this series is that I want each and every one to be SUPERB. I research them, compose my thoughts, discuss with other Aspies, discuss with my pet NTs, and then write them.

I'll let you in on a secret: Including this entry, there are 63 issues for The Care and Feeding of Your Aspie (Please note there are two issue 21s). I have written three times as many and discarded two thirds of them. I know, you have to be asking yourself – "HOW BAD WERE THE OTHERS IF THESE WERE THE BEST OF THEM!?" Let me tell you… They were bad.

And that's why I felt that this would be a good part of the series.

Not a day goes by that I don't write. Compulsively. I can't help it. And that is the way it is with special interests… we just do it.

Most people don't realize that there are a couple different kinds of special interests… Well, that's not true. There are a lot of kinds of special interests, but most of them can be relegated to one of three categories – Learning Interests, Collecting Interests and Skill Interests. I'll explain that a little.

Learning Interests:
Learning Interests are pretty simple. Your Aspie finds a topic of subject that GRABS his mind with an iron grip and won't let go. While the endorphins last your Aspie will absorb every piece of information on the topic that they can find. They will devour texts, websites, books, videos, DVDs, and input from experts in the field. Within a very short time, your Aspie will become a veritable expert on the subject. They can write essays, wikipedia articles or books on the topic. But it is all about the information and collecting it.

Collecting Interests:
Collecting Interests are a lot like Learning Interests – but it is things, not information that we have become fixated on. Whether it be My Little Pony, Star Wars Figures, or Skylanders, your Aspie will want EVERY ONE OF THEM. Comics, action figures, beanie babies… Anything that is limited edition and collectible can be the focus of a Collecting Interest.

Skill Interests:
These are, in my opinion, the interests that are most likely to be life long interests for your Aspie. Skill interests are a little hard to understand from within the Special Interest paradigm. Unlike the other types of interests – Skill Interests are all about DOING something. The following are examples of Skill

Interests (each of these is an example from Aspies I know or have spoken with) – Training Dogs; Making 2d JRPGs; Coding PHP for websites; Writing. These interests make your Aspie a highly skilled, specialist of an individual.

I have a few collecting interests, a few Information interests and a lot of skill interests… I don't know if that makes me odd – as Aspies go, or not.

I know I have talked about special interests and the need to encourage them in the past, but I cannot reiterate this need, enough. The pursuit of special interests is a mild or diluted OCD. They are Obsessive and Compulsory. If you have never experienced OCD, you really can't understand what it is like. I try not to minimize other people's experiences, but this is one time that I mean it… IF YOU'VE NEVER EXPERIENCED OCD, YOU CANNOT EVEN BEGIN TO GRASP WHAT IT IS LIKE.

This scene in Scrubs is pretty damn close, however. https://youtu.be/7kfLdwL1t98

Kevin Casey (Michael J. Fox's Character) could not stop washing his hands. I can't stop writing, looking for that last skylander, shooting films and the like. And your Aspie can't stop learning, talking about, collecting or doing whatever it is they do. We do what we do, because we have to some times.

The scene from scrubs is designed to evoke empathy for Kevin Casey. We don't need that empathy, we don't need someone to feel sorry for our interests. Unlike most OCD sufferers, we get the benefit of endorphins from it. So… revel in your Aspie's special interests… We do.

63 – The doomed land of Aspergia

This piece is controversial in nature. Many Aspies will disagree with the sentiments expressed in this article. I mean no disrespect, and like many of the articles in this series, I only speak for myself.

Aspergia – proper noun;
A fictional country that is characterized by citizenship that is comprised exclusively (or almost exclusively) of Aspies.

In reality, Aspergia is a thought experiment that has been tossed around by the Aspie community for several years. The first couple times that I came across the concept and topic, I was all for it. A country of, by and for Aspies! BRING IT ON!

Then I got to thinking about it. I mean, really thinking about it… And I don't think it would work.

First of all, I think it would be a racist country. I know what you are thinking, Aspies are human beings, right? That is true, but there are some MAJOR neurological differences between Aspies and Neurotypicals.

So, my take on it is that if we can state that someone with a different skin color is a different race (which is a purely cosmetic difference) – then we can state that Aspies are a different race. And as we can all agree on… I HOPE… Racism is a bad thing. Honestly, after pushing for neurodiversity, understanding, and acceptance for so long… to found a country that is Aspie only is a slap in the face of all those that have worked for our cause over the years. Exclusionism is just… not something that sits well with me.

While a lot of Aspies revel in the idea of Aspergia… a lot of us have been excluded our entire lives, and the thought that we would be in a situation that we would end up excluding an entire (LARGE) class of people, does not sit well. Most Aspies have a tendency towards fairness in their lives and there is nothing fair about excluding someone based on their genes.

That, right there, is another issue. A lot of people state that we don't know what causes Autistic Spectrum Disorders, but as studies progress, we are becoming more and more certain that it is a genetic disorder. That means that it has a biological source. Like many genetic disorders and diseases, we are not entirely certain what part of the genome causes it. In all likelihood, it is a combination of genetic markers that are in the on position.

Now. Think about this… Aspergia is a country by, for, and of Aspies… A country that is populated by Aspies… Some people argue for letting the NT spouses and and children of Aspies live in the country. Statistically speaking, this is a small number when compared to the numbers of Aspies.

So… with the very concept, we are setting up an Aspie breeding program. In essence, we would be putting a Eugenics Aspie Breeding program in place. After several generations, we will be guaranteeing that Asperger's will be breeding true within Aspergia's borders.

Why is this a bad thing?

Well… Think about the common perception of Aspies. We are considered rude, selfish, lacking empathy, and sometimes have violent outbursts, (Violent in the clinical sense of the word…I discuss that HERE.) have sensory issues, stim and worse at times… Now… think about the way that selection works.

Natural selection works by the simple fact that those that survive live to pass on their genetic code. In a country that is

JUST Aspies, (let's face it, the NT spouses and children of Aspies would not be that common in Aspergia) the process of un-natural selection would proceed at an accelerated pace. Literally, Aspergia would be a genetic factory, building a more concentrated type of Aspie. And honestly, eventually, the UN would sanction, Russia would invade and the United States would Nuke us – all to just shut us up… I mean, think about the foreign policy there… I can sum it up in four words – "You're doing it wrong." Let me tell you, world superpowers don't like hearing that.

Now… Let's look at jobs. When I've talked to psychiatric professionals, we've discussed the ideas of Aspies and jobs. There are a lot of jobs that Aspies are not cut out for, really.
- Factory Jobs – boring repetition with a LOT of noise and a LOT of icky, greasy dirty parts
- Retail – too many people
- Food service – too many people, hot, uncomfortable, greasy, and repetitious
- Waste treatment – smelly, dirty and icky

Pretty much anything that ever appeared on the show Dirty Jobs is a pretty bad job for an Aspie. I know, there are exceptions to this, but I do not think there are enough of the exceptions to cover these jobs. There are too many jobs necessary to keep a country running that Aspies are not cut out for… And you can't force Aspies to work them, even in the interests of keeping the country going.

There's also the concept of socializing. Many Aspies state that Aspies would be so happy because there would be no NTs forcing them to go out and socialize… The problem is, while we are a sub-species of human, we are still human… we are social creatures… even the most isolated of us needs socialization. We need interaction and input. Without it, we can go nuts… I mean literally…

So social interaction is necessary. There is a problem with this. Think about the problems with Aspies and NTs socializing. It's even worse with Aspies and Aspies. No, SERIOUSLY… Check out any of the forums dedicated to Autistic Spectrum Individuals and you will see what you mean. Honestly, unless Aspies share a special interest, the only they have in common is… Well… Asperger's Syndrome.

I could continue, but I am not sure I need to… With only Aspies, we won't have the workers to keep it going, no workers to make the infrastructure, a lack of socialization and the impending crushing war (and Aspie soldiers are not a threat, believe me) from the countries that we insult… Aspergia is doomed.